THE WORTH OF EVERY SOUL

Also by Steven A. Cramer

<u>Books</u>

Putting On The Armor of God

Conquering Your Own Goliaths

Great Shall Be Your Joy

In The Arms of His Love

Draw Near Unto Me

In His Image

<u>Fireside Recordings</u>

Conquering Your Own Goliaths

Winning the Battles with Satan

Angels: Messengers of God's Love

THE
WORTH OF
EVERY SOUL

Gerald & LoAnne Curtis

Formerly Steven A. Cramer

ISBN: 1-55517-726-3
e. 1

Published by Cedar Fort, Inc.
925 N. Main Springville, Ut., 84663
www.cedarfort.com

Distributed by:

Cover design by Nicole Cunningham
Cover design © 2004 by Lyle Mortimer

Printed in the United States of America
10 9 8 7 6 5 4 3 2 1

Printed on acid-free paper

Library of Congress Cataloging-in-Publication Data

Curtis, Gerald, 1938-
   The worth of every soul / Gerald & LoAnne Curtis.
        p. cm.
   Rev. ed. of: Cramer, Steven A. The worth of a soul. Orem, Utah : Randall Book, c1983.
   Includes bibliographical references.
   ISBN 1-55517-726-3 (pbk. : alk. paper)
   1. Curtis, Gerald, 1938- 2. Mormons--United States--Biography. I. Curtis, LoAnne. II.
Cramer, Steven A. Worth of a soul. III. Title.
   BX8695.C73A38 2004
   289.3'092--dc22

                                        2003027492

Remember
the worth of souls
is great in the sight of God;

And how great is his joy
in the soul that repenteth!

(D&C 18:10, 13)

To Don, Jeri, Janae, Tracy, Chad,
Tamara, Wendi, Karyn & Kristy

ACKNOWLEDGMENTS

This book would not be possible were it not for the example and support of our family, past and present. Worthy ancestors who preceded us paved the way for our deliverance from our own trials. Our living family, close and extended, sustained us in every way possible. We gratefully acknowledge their contribution to our eventual recovery.

We express our deepest gratitude to George Pace, who first opened my mind to the availability of Christ's power and grace as "the way" out of darkness and captivity. And to Charles Beckert who then helped my heart to soften so that I could be released from bondage to the past and accept Christ's way.

We owe a great debt of gratitude to all our friends of the former 17th and 26th wards in the Phoenix West Stake who stood by us and lent encouragement and support throughout most of the years of our trials.

We gratefully acknowledge all those who shared their hearts and their pains with us, for it was the discovery that their sorrows, problems and frustrations were so similar to ours that encouraged us to share what we have learned and gained through ours.

We deeply appreciate the staff at Cedar Fort for making this rewrite possible.

TABLE OF CONTENTS

PROLOGUE

In 1976 I was released from my calling as a bishop. I was living a clean and worthy life when I was called to serve in that position, and I continued to do so while I served in that office. But after I was released my life quickly fell apart and in less than two years I was excommunicated. This book will tell you why that happened and how it could have been prevented. It will explain how, as a young boy, my life got tangled up in sexual abuse and the subsequent addictive compulsions which eventually led to my excommunication and which almost destroyed our marriage. It will describe thirty years of failure as I struggled to overcome those addictions, with all the attendant despair and self-loathing.

And then you will read of the incredible rescue which I received from our Savior, Jesus Christ. In fact, I will tell you the entire story of my rescue from that life of failure, addiction, suicidal depression and shame, how He saved our marriage and our family, as well as how He helped my wife through the heartache I caused her. We will share with you the success story of how He changed my heart and my nature, setting me free from addiction, and giving us both a new life of freedom, peace, joy and self-respect so that we could experience His grace and grow in His love.

Most importantly, we will explain the gospel principles that make it possible for every person to experience the same kind of rescue and change of heart. My wife LoAnne will also explain how the Lord supported and sustained her as she suffered the abuse, betrayal and heartache which my sins imposed upon her for so many years, with the hope that those spouses who are currently suffering similar trials can find the help they need to journey through their pain.

I can still remember that early morning, as though it were yesterday, when I answered a knock on our front door. My heart pounded wildly and my hand trembled as I reached for the knob. Even though

I had been expecting this, and knew who it was, I opened the door with fear and apprehension. I glumly said good morning to my bishop and the high priest he had brought with him as "a second witness." There was an awkward silence as we stared at each other wordlessly. These were my brethren—men with whom I had prayed and served and counseled. But now I was without words to express my despair. The mixture of grief and pity that I saw in their faces manifested the intense discomfort which they felt on my behalf. They handed me an envelope from the stake president. I already knew what it contained: the summons—the summons to a church disciplinary council where the status of my membership would be decided. The procedures at that time required it to be delivered in person by "two trusted Melchizedek Priesthood holders" who could then stand as witnesses that the accused person was properly notified of the action pending. They stammered a few clumsy words, trying to express their regret, but soon turned awkwardly to leave, not really knowing what to say.

What *can* be said at a time such as this when, for one brief moment, time is frozen? A time when injured hearts are breaking and the heavens are weeping over the loss of another child of God. Weeping, not in condemnation or anger, but in the knowledge of the many heartaches to come, yet with that perfect and stubborn love which does not lessen—even in these unfortunate circumstances. For a brief moment, as I watched my brethren leave, I actually felt more sorrow for their pain than I did for my *own*. I shut the door and opened the letter, already knowing what it would say: "Dear Brother Curtis, You are hereby requested to appear before a high council court in the high council room for investigation of your conduct in violation of the law and order of the Church." The words blurred as bitter tears of remorse, confusion, and frustration flooded my eyes. With a trembling hand, I wiped the tears away and read the rest of the letter.

> You should be present with witnesses, if you desire them, at the time and place specified. If there is good reason why you cannot be present, please notify the undersigned in due time. In the event of your absence, without excuse, action must necessarily be taken in accordance with the evidence presented and the established procedure of the Church in such matters.

My excommunication process had begun. I thought I knew what it would mean to open the door and receive that summons, but I was wrong. As I finished reading the letter and the tears increased, I could hardly know that the intense anguish and torment which I felt at that moment, and which I had *already* caused in the hearts of my loved ones, had only *begun*. As I stared at those unbelievable words, I had absolutely no conception of the horrible struggle that lay ahead for myself and the loved ones I had betrayed. But Satan had been there before, with many other victims, and he knew very well the sorrow and heartache that was about to come into our family. Destroying marriages and families are among his greatest victories and I am certain that somewhere nearby he and his diabolical helpers were rejoicing over the delivery of that letter; rejoicing that they were about to receive yet another victim of their deceiving lies and skillful manipulations. After twenty-eight years of struggle to gain my soul, he was at last going to have me fully within the grasp of his evil power. Because he had finally persuaded me to violate sacred temple covenants, I was about to be expelled from the Church and kingdom of God—the Church which I had loved and spent all my life serving to the best of my ability; the Church on which I had turned my back and polluted with deliberate sin of the most serious nature; the Church which would now be required by the laws of God to expel one who had broken solemn temple vows and deliberately violated sacred covenants between himself, his God and his spouse.

Yes, Satan was most surely rejoicing, certain that he had won. But Satan was wrong. His victory would only be *temporary*. It was true that he now had me wrapped securely in the chains of hell. But unknown to me, the Savior was already planning my rescue! Now that I know Him better, I realize one of the main things Christ does is to plan the rescue of those who are willing to be rescued. He will rescue them not only from their sins and addictions, not only from weaknesses and bad habits, but also from broken hearts and broken relationships. His rescue extends to *every* heartache, resentment and negative emotion which keeps us from believing and receiving His love and healing forgiveness which is so abundantly available if we will only accept it.

At that time, after a lifetime of sexual addiction and failure to live up to the spiritual standards taught by the Church, it was beyond my belief or comprehension that I could ever become clean, pure, or acceptable to the Lord. I had no understanding of what it means when the Lord changes your heart and makes you *new*. At that time I could neither understand nor conceive the freedom, joy and resulting feelings of self-worth that are possible when we allow God to change our hearts and our natures, transforming us beyond the carnal nature of our fallen flesh. At that time, my perceptions of being obedient were based only on what I could do to restrain my evil desires with my limited willpower and self-discipline which, (after twenty-eight years of failure) I already knew were unquestionably inadequate to overcome my sinfulness or to make me worthy before the Lord.

As the Lord guided us through the coming years, my wife and I would both learn that *nothing* is impossible for Christ if we will allow Him to do His work within us. The time would come when I would be delivered from my sinful addictions by the majesty and power of His redeeming love and Atonement. Before this horrible experience was over, I would learn that it is never too late to repent. By the time I was fully rescued, I knew that absolutely everyone who will respond to the Atonement is within the reach of Christ's perfect, unconditional, and unwavering love. I think, as I wept and stared at that letter, that somewhere in the heavenly courts above, the beautiful words of the Savior to His grieving Apostles were echoing again: "Ye shall weep and lament ... and ye shall be sorrowful, but your sorrow shall be turned into joy" (John 16:20).

In the original book, *The Worth of A Soul*, I described the things we experienced through my years of addiction, the excommunication, my recovery and rescue. However, looking back twenty-five years later, I realize that the picture I painted was not complete, for we had not yet stepped back far enough to appreciate its full significance. Since that original version of our story was published, we have met many who continue to struggle through addiction, broken marriages and despair because they do not know how to come to Christ to be rescued.

It has been our privilege to work with hundreds of individuals and families who have experienced defeats similar to ours. We deeply appreciate the trust these people have placed in us, and the insights they have provided by sharing their struggles with us. Through them we have learned that the path to rescue and victory is seldom the same for any two people or families. This is because we all come to Him with differing needs, backgrounds, weaknesses and failures. But there are basic principles that apply to all of us; key ingredients that can guide us in our individual paths to the Savior. We also come to Him with different misconceptions, weaknesses of faith and common barriers of unbelief and doubt that must be overcome before we can part the veil to grasp that divine hand that will lift us beyond the fallen, carnal flesh.

We will attempt to identify all these processes as we have come to understand them through our own experience.

We have been led to an increased understanding of Satan's power to deceive and manipulate. More importantly, we are convinced of Christ's power to heal and rescue individuals, families, and marriages, no matter how long they have been in Satan's grasp, no matter how completely they have been enslaved and no matter how deeply the wounds were inflicted. We have experienced the lifting, changing power of His infinite Atonement and know that it brings great joy and peace to the suffering soul. And we know that when proper principles and faith in Christ are applied, the "natural-man" dilemmas that keep so many of us from obtaining victory will be overcome.

Because God never changes and because He is no respecter of persons, His blessings are equally available for every person. Thus, the personal journey of discovery and rescue we will describe is available to every reader. It is our earnest desire that by sharing what we have learned during the last twenty-five years, others might also experience our Savior's mercy.

Since that first publication, we have been besieged with requests for more information from my wife. I appreciate her valuable insight and aid in this retelling. You will recognize her text by the following font:

When I look back over my life and its trials and adversity, I don't see anything that is earth-shakingly different from anyone else's trials and sufferings. We are all sent here to learn and grow through the things we suffer. Your pain may originate from a different trial than mine, but we all experience pain. And the grand purpose of pain is to bring us to Christ.

For some, coming to Christ is a sudden, revelatory experience, while for others it is a gradual, step-by-step process. But for all of us, the goal is the same. Your life's experiences may be more valid and valuable in helping another person than mine. But, because I believe we must all reach out to each other in an effort to come to Christ together, I am willing to share my pain and my progress along that path if someone else may benefit by it. To that end I am willing to relate some of the principles I have learned and the insights I have gained on our mutual telestial trek of tears. This is also an opportunity for me to bear unwavering testimony that, after all we can do, it is Christ who brings us home.

Note: All italic emphasis in quotations are the author's emphasis unless otherwise noted in the citation.

CHAPTER ONE

HOW I GOT INTO TROUBLE

The seeds of addiction which led to my excommunication were planted by the sexual abuse I encountered as a young boy. To explain how an innocent boy with a strong Latter-day Saint family background fell into a life of immorality that eventually led to suicidal despair and then excommunication, this chapter is divided into five sections: the sexual abuse that was *the origin* of my problems with sexual addiction, the *consequences* of the choices I made in regard to that addiction, how the addiction *escalated* in spite of my efforts to stop, the various *things I tried* to overcome the addiction, and the *things we have learned* looking back from a perspective of twenty-five years later.

ORIGINS

As a child, I was taught the gospel in the home and was expected to live it. I think I did a pretty good job of it until age twelve, when I was sexually abused by my father's friend and employer. He taught me to masturbate, a practice that was completely unknown to me until then. There had been other relatives and friends(?) of the family who had abused me sexually before this man, and there would be more in my later teenage years, but this was the pivotal event, because he told me this secret practice was something that must be taught to all boys to develop their manhood. He ordered me to never reveal or discuss this practice with my parents—an order most abusers give to their child victims. He persuaded me to keep it a secret by convincing me that it would be terribly embarrassing and humiliating to my father to have to discuss such things because my dad, being crippled with polio, was "not fully a man." He claimed that he was doing my father a favor by explaining this to me for him. Nevertheless, my conscience warned me that something was wrong with this man's instructions, and after his initial introduction, I abstained from the practice of it for a long time.

Eventually, however, the day came when natural urges and the curiosity of puberty overcame my apprehension. It is significant that the first time I decided to perform this act on my own, I distinctly heard a voice from the other side of the veil warn me not to do so, but to go and discuss it with my father.

Oh, how I wish I had heeded that warning! But I did not. Instead, I chose to go ahead and experiment. That single act of disobedience was soon followed by another, and another, until it eventually grew beyond a youthful habit to become a compulsive addiction, an obsessive behavior which would dominate my life and keep me enslaved through thirty years of heartache and despair.

CONSEQUENCES OF MY CHOICES

Even though the spiritual dangers and consequences of masturbation were never discussed in my home or priesthood classes, this secret habit made me feel dirty. As the years passed and I became more and more dependent upon the practice, my feelings of guilt also grew, creating within me a haunting sense of inferiority. I avoided friendships. I never felt worthy or comfortable with others. I learned to distance myself so that no one could ever get close enough to discover my dark secret.[1]

At the end of high school I received an academic scholarship to our local college, but having no goals or ideas about what to do with my life, I decided to join the Air Force. Since I grew up in various small towns, I never had the opportunity to attend seminary, but in the Air Force I discovered a love for the scriptures and I began to rapidly grow and mature in the gospel. In the first six months, I read the standard works from cover to cover. The spiritual strength I gained was a great help in trying to overcome my habit. And the closer I grew to the Lord through prayer and the scriptures, the greater the guilt I felt whenever I indulged in the practice. Then, two years after joining the Air Force, I married a girl I had known for just a few months during the first part of my senior year of high school. Not only were we very young, immature and ill-prepared for the adjustments required in a normal marriage, we were completely unprepared for the trials that lay ahead because of my addiction to masturbation.

---

1 Such damage to important relationships is one of the worst consequences of secret sexual sin.

ESCALATION

I had expected that marital sex would bring an end to my addiction, but to my surprise and confusion, the compulsion for this act of self-abuse actually increased. I can now understand why that was so. Because of the feelings of inferiority and guilt which had accumulated during the previous eight years of shame, I not only found it difficult to *give* LoAnne honest affection, but also to *receive* the love she tried to give me. The resulting loneliness, confusion and discouragement continued to drive me back to the same form of self-gratification time after time.

Then, for the first time in my life, I discovered pornographic magazines and everything changed. Viewing these presentations of nudity fueled my lust beyond anything I had ever fantasized. It added a new and obsessive dimension to the temporary comfort and escape which my previous self-abuse had provided. I was now caught by a filthiness and more powerful carnality than had ever been there before.[2] As my dependence upon pornography grew, the addiction developed so much power over me that I was constantly vulnerable to it, even when it was not part of my thoughts or intent. For example, every time I felt lonely or discouraged, if LoAnne and I had an argument, if I saw a pin-up, or even if I noticed someone else looking at a pornographic magazine, my body would start shaking and I'd break into a cold sweat. My face would turn white and my heart would pound wildly. I would find myself seized with an overwhelming compulsion to indulge in that vile trash, consumed with desires which I had not planned or chosen. Like an alcoholic or drug addict, I was "hooked," believing the delusion of every addict that indulgence would somehow ease the pain and make me happy.

I tried very hard to overcome these two rapidly growing addictions. Sometimes, by setting goals and making endless promises to myself and to God, there were times when I withheld myself from sin for several months at a time, and this was wonderful. But during those periods of abstinence, the *other* part of me, the rotten part that loved the sin, would be growing stronger and more insistent. The pressure to give in was like water building up behind a faulty dam. The longer I abstained, the greater the pressure I felt to give in and the weaker I

---

2   This may seem strange in today's world of easy Internet, cable and satellite access to pornography, but such things were not available during my years of addiction.

grew. No matter how hard I tried to prevent it, sooner or later my resolve would weaken, the dam of my resistance would crack, and the accumulated pressure of months of abstinence would wash my willpower away in another flood of indulgence.

Sometimes I could resist these diabolical attacks, but even when I was successful in a temporary resistance, I would be haunted by it for days, wondering what I had missed. For example, one morning some years later, I got up early to do some yard work. As I took my first load of trimmings to the alley, I found two discarded pornographic magazines lying on the ground behind our fence. I immediately began to shake and tremble, filled with an overwhelming desire to pore over the nudity I knew would be displayed therein. Somehow I managed to throw them into the bottom of the garbage dumpster and bury them under the trimmings. That should have been a victory. But the carnal part of me was so terribly haunted by what I had missed in those magazines that within a few days I gave way to the pressure of desire and fell into another cycle of indulgence.

When I lost control and gave in, I often went on pornographic binges, much like an alcoholic who goes back to drink after a period of abstinence. Sometimes I could throw off these devastating cycles of surrender in only a few days, but often they extended to several weeks of rampant lust. But eventually I'd become so saturated with the filth that it became abhorrent and disgusting to me. Overpowered by self-loathing and shame, I hated myself for what I was doing and for what it was doing to me. Somehow that self-disgust and guilt would give me the strength to throw it off and begin another cycle of repentance.

I cannot adequately describe the fear and helpless insecurity I felt as I found myself being swept away by desires and compulsions that had grown beyond my personal power to resist. Now I understand that is the nature of addiction. These problems did not persist because I didn't care or didn't try hard enough. Even though there was a part of me that was content to continue in the sin, I, the spirit person inside, the real me was determined to conquer this monster and live worthy of the celestial kingdom at all costs. But, while my periods of repentance were sincerely genuine and fraught with great shame and remorse, the temporary "high" produced by the evil combination of pornography and masturbation made it seem worth any price that must be paid. As the years passed, I became a living "Doctor Jekyll and Mr. Hyde" kind of person in my cycles of indulgence and repentance.

I felt desperate because of this emotional roller-coaster ride. It is a horrible way to live. I struggled for another twenty years trying to overcome or manage that double life.

THINGS I TRIED

I tried everything I could think of to overcome the evil that was controlling my life. I attended all my church meetings regularly. I immersed myself in the scriptures and church work to the point of fanaticism. I loved my opportunities for service in the church and served faithfully in many positions, including four stake missions. For most of the addiction years I read the four standard works cover to cover each year. But I didn't know back then that merely reading the words will not change you until you add faith to the promises you read. Marking the interesting verses will not change you either. Though my mortal eyes were scanning the promises of deliverance, my spirit was blind to their real message, the message that only Jesus Christ could save me from the spiritual prison that was binding me with the chains of hell. I also fasted frequently and prayed constantly for deliverance. As sincere as those prayers were, however, in my ignorance of the Savior's power to change my nature, those thirty years of prayers were little more than desperate begging. They were not the prayers of faith which can pull down the powers of heaven, because they were not based with confidence in what the Savior has revealed He can do to free people from such situations.

During my cycles of repentance I also read dozens of motivational, therapy and self-help books to try and understand myself and to learn how "the experts" could help me to overcome my compulsions. These philosophies of men were helpful because they taught me how our attitudes and thought processes relate to behavior. I learned about the powerful, self-defeating effect which a negative, failure-focused mind can have on our beliefs and expectations. So I set goals and tried to fill my life with positive affirmations. I still benefit from doing that today. For example, one of my favorite affirmations is: "My body is a temple and my mind is the holy of holies." Another is: "I am a disciple of Christ, therefore, I will never deliberately choose to do something that would disappoint Him." I hope I never stop using such positive input, but I now understand why man's wisdom and willpower, unaided by Christ, will never be enough to change a heart or a fallen nature.

Over the years I have come to understand that there is a danger in relying too much on the wisdom of men, because all those terrestrial philosophies of "positive thinking" are designed to build faith in our *own* power rather than Christ's. Of course it is important to have self-confidence and positive expectations, because, as someone said, "The will to do something springs from the knowledge or confidence that we *can* do it." But one of the most difficult lessons for the natural man or woman to learn is that the confidence to live worthily must be based in Christ and His power, rather than in our own limited abilities, because "there is no flesh that can dwell in the presence of God, save it be through the merits, and mercy, and grace of the Holy Messiah" (2 Nephi 2:8).

I can now see that many aspects of those self-development books were harmful to me because they fed my delusion that somehow, if I learned enough, if I persisted long enough and tried hard enough, someday I would triumph and heal myself of this evil part of my nature. I have seen this same mistake made by hundreds of other determined, well-meaning people. This seems to be a mistake typical of the natural-man's prideful expectation of fixing himself instead of allowing his weaknesses to teach him to rely upon the Lord. Perhaps that is why Alma counseled his son, Helaman, "Teach them to withstand every temptation of the devil, with their faith on the Lord Jesus Christ" (Alma 33:37). And perhaps that is why he taught his son, Shiblon, (and us) the spiritual formula that "as much as ye shall put your trust in God even so much ye shall be delivered out of your trials, and your troubles, and your afflictions . . ." (Alma 38:5). As Paul said:

> And my speech and my preaching was not with enticing words of man's wisdom, but in demonstration of the spirit and of power: That *your faith should not stand in the wisdom of men*, but in the power of God (1 Corinthians 2:4-5).

Eventually, with increasing resolve and self-discipline, my periods of abstinence lasted longer and the cycles of indulgence grew further apart. I found myself serving in positions of increasingly higher responsibilities within the Church and I loved it. But the righteous times were always haunted by the threat of that ever-increasing pressure behind the faulty dam of my limited willpower. Because I had not yet received the mighty change of heart that comes through the "born again" process, deep inside there was still that fallen, carnal part of me that loved the sin. Eventually, no matter how hard I struggled to resist, the evil on the inside would win, and I would plunge into another cycle of sin. As the years passed, the cyclical addiction grew more powerful and frightening, because each time I fell, my indulgence went deeper and lasted longer than before. Every time I fell, another part of me died. Each fall destroyed more of my self-image.[3] The shame and insecurity were devastating. It became more and more difficult for me to decide which part of me was Doctor Jekyll and which part was Mr. Hyde. It became harder and harder to hope that I could ever conquer myself.

CONCLUSIONS—WHAT I HAVE LEARNED

My torturous up-and-down cycles lasted through twenty years of marriage and eight children. During all this time, LoAnne did what she could to support me, trying to understand and help. In spite of the incredible pain this betrayal inflicted on her, she was patient and forgiving. But it was not a problem that she could solve for me. Whether it is drugs, alcohol or pornography, no wife can solve such problems for her husband. There would be many bitter lessons before I would finally learn that it was also not a problem which *I*, an imperfect, fallen being could solve either, because spiritual death can never restore life to itself. Indeed, my addiction would never be conquered until I learned how to turn it over to the Savior and *His* power.

There really were two parts of me, both fighting for mastery. The first and most important part was the eternal, but now very wounded spirit. That part of me was determined to conquer this addiction and live worthy of the celestial kingdom. But deep inside there was also another part of me that was equally determined to continue in the sin. That second part was the fallen part of me, the "natural-man" part which made *me*, the spirit person inside, vulnerable to the carnal lusts which held me in a prison of uncontrollable desires. At that time I did not understand that this dual existence is a normal part of mortality and is the same conflict every mortal being faces as part of their probation, whether in addiction or not. I did not understand that we all *inherit* a fallen nature and vulnerability to sin just by being born as a descendent of Adam, so I made the mistake many of us make: I added to my problems by condemning myself for my vulnerability instead of turning to the Savior for the rescue and change of nature which He is so eager to provide.

---

3 Struggling wih a poor self-image is not limited to excommunicants or people in addiction. For more information see "The Goliath of a Poor Self Image" in *Conquering Your Own Goliaths*.

Eventually I would learn that only God has the power to change our hearts and fallen natures so that we no longer need or want improper behaviors. Eventually I would add my witness to that of King Benjamin's converts, who testified "the Spirit of the Lord Omnipotent . . . has wrought a mighty change in us, or in our hearts, that *we have no more disposition* to do evil, but to do good continually" (Mosiah 5:2). I had read those words many times. I even had them underlined, but I was blind to the essential steps that must come before any of us can receive that precious and mighty change of heart and nature. First must come the recognition that we can never save ourselves, that we must all surrender our needs to a higher power. "And they had viewed themselves in their own carnal state, even less than the dust of the earth" (Mosiah 4:2). I was an expert in that part. I was a master at admitting my sin and beating on myself for my filthiness and unworthiness. But I always got stuck there and it would be many years before I could move beyond that focus to the fulcrum which King Benjamin's people described in the rest of the same verse:

> And they had *viewed themselves* in their own carnal state, even less than the dust of the earth. And they all cried aloud with one voice, saying: O have mercy, and *apply* the atoning blood of Christ [to us] that we may receive forgiveness of our sins, and our hearts may be purified; for we believe in Jesus Christ, the son of God (Mosiah 4:2).

But at that time I was blind to His power to help me change and become what He wanted me to be. I was buried in filth and degradation. I was forty years old and fighting the same battle I had begun at the age of twelve. I was without hope because I was enslaved by an evil that had grown beyond my power to resist. I was without hope because I could not think of a single thing I could do that I had not already tried over and over during all those dark, dark years. When would this struggle end? Time was running out. In this state of hopeless despair, I was about to encounter the next major change in my life, a change that would break every heart and wound every soul who had stood with me through all those trying years.[4]

---

4 The reader should understand that in today's society, there is nothing unique about the two addictions that held me prisoner. Unfortunately, the abusive self-gratification of masturbation and pornography have become two of Satan's most common and deadly weapons, causing tremendous heartache to the person who misuses the sacredness of his or her mind and body, as well as the loved ones who struggle to understand and forgive the problem. Over the last twenty-five years there have

been hundreds who have shared with us similar stories of broken lives and marriages from the addiction to pornography. Our Church leaders are totally correct when they warn us, with increasing emphasis and frequency, that pornography is just as addictive and destructive as drugs and alcohol, if not even more so. Feeding upon its own awful lust, the viewing of pornography creates an ever-increasing hunger for more filth. Like a runaway cancer, it is never satisfied, but demands more and more of our time and passion until the victim can scarcely think of anything else and becomes willing to abandon everything of importance just to satisfy the cravings.

CHAPTER TWO

EARLY MARRIAGE YEARS

I was very young and starry-eyed when I got married. The old joke about marrying for a little cottage with green shutters and a white picket fence around it with the patter of happy little feet inside was exactly true of me. More than anything, I wanted to be a "mommy" and raise the ideal Latter-day Saint family. I was barely seventeen when we were engaged, and so naive, but thought I was capable of conquering the world—my world at least.

Gerald confessed his problem with masturbation to me shortly after we were engaged, but naive as I was, I didn't understand it. Plus, we both were convinced the problem would cease to exist after we were married. So, even though I sensed it was terrible, I never spoke about it to my parents because it was important to me to live what I perceived to be the ideal image of a Latter-day Saint couple. My ideals first clashed with reality in the week after our engagement. I accompanied him from my home in New Mexico to Arizona for a visit with his family. While there, I could tell his desires for me were mostly sexual, but instead of heeding the warning flags that such a perception raised, I was excited to be the object of his desire, and I didn't realize it should be any different. "The world is too much with us," someone has said, and it was with me. The world justifies the sharing of passion before marriage and it was too easy for us to justify it as well. It was fortunate for both of us that Gerald left a week after our engagement or we may have entirely lost our virtue.

He was in the Air Force and was stationed halfway across the United States in Minnesota. His letters all spoke of how hard he was working to become worthy of a temple marriage. His frank descriptions of his attempts to be clean and free of the addictive habit embarrassed me. It made me feel uncomfortable to read his letters. We had to postpone our marriage date once because of his unsuccessful struggle with his habit. I allowed my family to think the postponement was because he couldn't get time off from the Air Force.

Finally the day came when he felt he was ready to answer all the temple recommend questions affirmatively and honestly. Once again the date was set and this time invitations were sent. He got leave from the Air Force and drove non-stop from Minnesota to New Mexico to meet me and take me to the temple. After we were married, we excitedly packed our possessions and headed off in our second-hand car to make our first home in a little town called Peculiar, Missouri, near the base Gerald was temporarily assigned to in Kansas City. I was in my element– making a home out of the apartment we rented. I was very happy, except for Gerald's incessant desire and never-ending demands for sex. I was confused by it and by what my role should be. I wanted to help and to acquiesce to his constant requests, but it was too much. And I didn't know how to say no in a way that he would accept without it seeming to be a cruel rejection. My love for him, as new as it was, became clouded by the embarrassment I felt over the inconvenient and overriding need he exhibited. I felt caught in a web I didn't understand or comprehend. I knew this problem must be related to his former obsession, and that he expected me to be a substitute for that habit, but I was beginning to realize I couldn't fill his expectations. However, it took many more years before I finally understood that the problem of his needs had grown far beyond anything that could be influenced by what I did or did not do.

It is very common in such relationships that the sexual addict blames his partner for his unfulfilled, lustful "needs." When she doesn't perform as often or in the manner he desires, then he is thwarted in his obsession and it is easy for him to think she is cold and uncaring, or that he must have married the wrong person. It is important to realize that these "needs" of his are motivated by lust, not love. And that dehumanizes the woman and turns her into an object of lust rather than a cherished person with needs of her own for love and respect. The man that has become enslaved to pornography will never find a living, breathing woman who can consistently fulfill his fantasies, or live up to his sexual expectations in a long-term relationship. But it was many years before we realized the truth of our situation. Instead, I lived with a growing sense of inadequacy and he felt more and more cheated.

After six weeks in Missouri, Gerald was transferred back to Minnesota. We had wonderful times there as we participated in that little branch of the Church. We met in a house that had been converted to a chapel with basement classrooms. Our numbers were few, but the branch members were a close, family-like group. I was given callings and opportunities to serve in every organization, sometimes in multiple capacities. But I had little else to do and I was very happy learning to serve in adult capacities. Gerald and I were struggling to make a good, happy relationship, and had no doubt that we would. His sexual needs continued to wear on me, and I felt increasingly inadequate. However, my overriding concern at this time was the fact that I had not conceived a child. A whole year went by, then part of another, and I was at times driven to tears over the seemingly interminable wait. Then, just a few months before Gerald's four-year tour in the Air Force expired, I learned I was, indeed, with child. At last I would be a mommy!

At the end of his enlistment in 1960, we traveled back to New Mexico where we moved into a little one-bedroom apartment on my family's property. Gerald worked that summer at my dad's business and I spent a lot of time with my family. In fact, it was too much time because my allegiance became blurred and I found it easy to retreat to the comfort of my parents' family when things were difficult between Gerald and me. And then, with the added discomfort and hormonal changes in my body, coexistence became very difficult between us. I no longer had the slightest inclination for sex—and that is all it had become because of his ongoing, and ever-increasing demands. Unbeknownst to me, he had by this time begun to use pornography. The Spirit was driven away from our home and replaced with anger and heated words. It was there, in that tiny apartment that we began to accept a lesser standard of behavior; that of yelling and hurtful verbal exchanges that soon became the norm when one of us felt hurt or slighted by the other.

If I could give one piece of advice to newly-married couples it would be this: Set a high standard by which you will behave toward your spouse and never allow yourself to fall below it. Don't let hurt, stress, or misunderstandings allow you to justify unbecoming behavior, for it is terribly easy to make it a habit. Hold yourself strictly to a high standard of words and actions. Be honest and humble in the expression of your feelings—never accusative or retaliative. Shun the use of sarcasm. Never raise your voice, because if you do, that is what will become the focus of attention rather than the problem that caused it in the first place. It also allows the other person to justify whatever unkind words or actions caused your voice to be raised against them.

That is what happened with us. As Gerald began to use pornography more and more, he tried to cover his feelings of guilt and shame by prodding me to become angry and raise my voice against him. When I responded in that manner, he felt justified in the sins he was committing, as if "I was driving him to it." It was to become a pattern. But I didn't understand any of that then. I was still very young and somewhat self-centered. Some of the things he said to me seemed deliberately intended to hurt and demean me, but in the foolishness of youth, I never dreamed that was actually so. I thought it was cruel, but unintentional, and that he should see by my extreme reactions what it was doing to me. It was many years before I could conquer myself enough to refrain from such angry, overly vocal responses. Since then, I have learned that the best response to someone who seems to be striking out at you is quietness and an honest expression of your own feelings rather than retaliating with counter accusations. Perhaps if I'd responded that way in the beginning Gerald would have been forced to face his problems a lot sooner.

We left New Mexico in time for Gerald to enroll in a technical school and study electronics in Arizona starting in the fall. In December I gave birth to our first child, a son. We both took enormous joy in parenting this "perfect" child. And only eleven months later, we became parents of a wonderful daughter. I thought those were very happy days. Gerald was called to serve a stake mission and was busily engaged in the Lord's work. However, he was also enduring his cycles of evil, and on those occasions life between the two of us was miserable. I didn't know why those cycles happened. I just chalked our difficulties up to immaturity and selfishness and tried to do better. But my overriding memories of that time are happy— I was living my dream of motherhood and finding great joy in my children and my own service in the Church.

After completing his electronics course, Gerald obtained a job in the aerospace industry. During the next several years our family grew in size and we purchased our first home. I was mostly unaware of the spiritual battle Gerald was waging because we seldom talked about it. Occasionally he slipped, but most of the time he kept himself on course and served with distinction in his Church callings. Neither of us realized that Satan's trap was being slowly closed around him. We were both confident that, with more effort and resolve, he could overcome this terrible habit. (At this time, neither of us had realized that it was an addiction.) In fact, I believe we were doing so well that Satan found it necessary to use additional means of getting us in his clutches, or at least to accelerate the process, for it was about this time that Gerald listened to a presentation that convinced him there was a better way to make money, perhaps to even become rich in terms of worldly goods. Back in those days, pyramid schemes were not always recognized as such, but as wonderful "ground floor" business opportunities. Without realizing this great "business opportunity" he was interested in was nothing but a clever pyramid scheme, he quit his job. We sold our home and moved far away to south Texas.

There were many good things that happened to us in Texas, which make me very glad we had that experience, but improved finances was not one of them. Instead, we incurred a great debt, all the while moving up in the company and garnering the honor and recognition of others involved in the scheme. It didn't take long, however, for the government to realize what this company was doing and soon they began to prosecute. For that reason, Gerald left the company and we moved to Utah. By this time we had no monetary resources and were deeply in debt. He got a menial job selling hearing aids at Sears and we struggled. We were forced to call upon Church and family resources to help. The stress and struggle to support his family under such circumstances were active agents in causing him to revert to old habits—to seek solace and comfort from the wrong source. As he does with so many of us, Satan took advantage of these circumstances to confuse Gerald and drive him ever further from stability and normalcy.

As difficult as those times were financially, my memories of them include our growing family (we had six children), the joy I felt in the normal, day-to-day experiences with them, and my growing testimony that God knew me, loved me and heard my prayers. It was at this time that I had opportunity to bear my testimony that, in spite of our difficult financial circumstances, I absolutely knew the Church is true and that God loved and cared for me. And as I bore that testimony, I felt the Spirit envelop my entire being with that absolute knowledge. I wouldn't trade that experience, and others like it, for anything!

Then Gerald had an opportunity to sell encyclopedias and children's books. He did very well and we were able to resolve most of our debt, but it required him to be "on the road" much of the time. His best prospects were in little towns where people didn't have a lot of access to libraries, etc. (This was before Internet access.) After he exhausted most of the little towns in and around Utah, we decided to move back to Arizona, hoping he could do as well there. We rented a little house with a postage stamp-size yard and moved in with our soon-to-be-seven children. Financially, it didn't turn out to be as good a move as we had hoped, but we were making it. And Gerald had a renewed desire to be righteous and to serve the Lord. He enjoyed the longest cycle of righteousness and spirituality he'd ever had in his life.

During this time he was called to be bishop of our new ward. We both felt this was a confirmation of our belief that the moral struggles of the past must surely be over—and they were for the entire time he served as bishop of that ward. This was surely a blessing given through the grace of God incident to his faithful performance in that office. We both enjoyed some wonderful experiences during the time we lived there. We made good friends, enjoyed our callings and felt the Spirit in our lives and in our home as never before. It was a good time in every way but financially. Due to the time requirements of his bishop responsibilities, Gerald was not able to travel as much. Sales in our own city became more difficult and our income dropped below what we could survive on. We had hoped the Lord would prepare the means that Gerald could continue on in his calling, but it became increasingly clear it was not to be.

During a period of praying and pondering this problem, Gerald related to me that on Sunday, while conducting a ward council meeting, he perceived the bishop's mantle was lifted from him and placed upon another man in the room. It was so real to him that he suddenly felt like an imposter in the position. When he expressed his feelings to the stake president, he learned he had also been receiving promptings that Gerald should be released. It was no surprise to us that a few weeks later the other man was sustained as the new bishop of the ward.

I was devastated by his release. I couldn't understand why the Lord wouldn't bless us in such a way that we could continue serving Him as we'd been called to do. I had no idea, then, that this release might be a blessing in preventing a serious transgression while in his calling. It had been so long since he'd transgressed morally that we both were convinced those things were permanently behind us. After his release, however, we found out how wrong that assumption was. The cycles of sin swept back over him with a vengeance. I remember how disappointed and discouraged I felt when he first told me he'd done something wrong. I don't even remember exactly what it was, but we were amazed that it had happened and felt terrible about it. I was convinced he really meant it when he said it was a "one-time" lapse and he'd never do it again. It wasn't long, however, before he had another lapse.

The third time this happened, he didn't even have the courage to tell me himself, but asked a visiting friend, in whom he'd confided, to tell me. He probably hoped it would protect him from feeling my dismay, but I felt even more betrayed and disillusioned because I had to hear it from someone else. After that he mostly kept the cycles to himself, unless he felt he was over it, and could promise me "it would never happen again." Each time he told me that, I believed him and hoped for the best. It always encouraged me that he was willing to continue trying to overcome himself, that he continued to have a testimony of the gospel and that he continued in his appreciation for me and for his children. Because of those things I continued to believe he would become the "noble son of God" that my patriarchal blessing told me I would marry.

CHAPTER THREE

FROM BAD TO WORSE

No one jumps from being active in the Church to an excommunication in one giant leap. These awful tragedies come into one's life as the natural result of a series of compromises and improper choices. As Melvin J. Ballard said: "The most favorite method the enemy of our souls has employed in ages past and that he will employ today is to capture souls by leading them gently, step by step. Men and women do not go far wrong in an instant. It is by slow degrees, step by step" (*The New Era*, Mar. 1984, p. 38-39).

Although adultery is one of the most common weapons used to destroy marriages, Satan is far too clever to just come right out with the suggestion. He knows that adultery and broken marriages are far more likely if he leads us gradually, incrementally toward it, so slowly that we are unaware of the increasing peril we bring upon ourselves as we compromise our covenants and the loyalty we owe to our spouse. And so he begins slowly, first by drawing our attention away from the good characteristics of our spouse and getting us to focus on their weaknesses and flaws. He is a master at stirring up contention and dissatisfaction with our marriage relationship. (See 3 Nephi 11:29; Helaman 16:22.) If we are not carefully attentive to nourishing our marriage, we unwittingly cooperate with his plan, making our emotional soil fertile for straying into compromises and choices that lead us toward the illusion of pornography or other illicit relationships. Without even realizing it, we can descend step-by-step toward the emotions and transgressions that cause us to abandon our covenants and responsibilities. As this descent continues over weeks and months, we lose the Spirit, our thinking becomes distorted and we lose perspective. Our values and priorities begin to erode. As I have looked back upon the events which led to my fall, I have identified many pivotal points of decision where improper choices turned me downward and away from God toward the greedy clutches of Satan.

Through all those past years of lust and fantasy, as I had tried to avoid facing the difficulties and frustrations in our marriage, I sometimes indulged the fantasy of a better life with another companion. I had often thought of divorce as an easier way out. But did I ever once believe I could commit adultery? No! Not a fragment of a chance. I never dreamed it was even possible that I could ever "go all the way" and have a relationship with a real person other than my wife. That was forbidden. It was unthinkable. It would be the sin "next to murder." (See Alma 39:5; *Mormon Doctrine*: Adultery, p. 23.) Yet, I was all the while freely and naively indulging in rampant mental adultery without expecting the inevitable consequence.

Hundreds of other excommunicants have disclosed to me the same naive pride of fallen man, being equally deceived by the same Satanic delusion that they could flirt with someone, or tamper with pornography without going all the way. "*I thought I could handle it*," is probably the most common excuse heard in church disciplinary councils. The reason we can't "handle it" is that each compromise makes the next one easier and incrementally larger. Gradually, carnal pleasures or stolen affections seem to be more important than covenants, loyalty and honor, until finally, there will not be even a hesitation before the ultimate sin of adultery. Because of Satan's patient and carefully worked skills, the unthinkable will be done. "And others will he pacify, and lull them away into carnal security, that they will say: All is well in Zion; yea, Zion prospereth, all is well—and thus the devil cheateth their souls, and leadeth them away carefully down to hell" (2 Nephi 28:21).

This diabolical process is exemplified by our experience. There were four specific situations that led to my fall and excommunication. The first was doing nothing to correct the indifference I felt toward what I believed to be an empty marriage relationship. Then I allowed excessive debt and financial burdens to erode my spirituality. When I gave up the struggle against my addictions, dropping out of church followed naturally.

1. SURRENDERING THE MARRIAGE

I think we would have been ill-equipped to fulfill each other's needs under the best of circumstances, but with the complications of my periodic return to pornography and masturbation, with the shame and emptiness I felt, we faced problems that would have challenged the best of relationships. Consequently, after we were married, I often felt loneliness, disappointment and resentment for what I thought were my wife's failures as my companion. And as she described in the previous chapter, my hollow emptiness and inability to give and receive love left her feeling inadequate and used. I can now see that all those invisible barriers she built around her tender emotions were necessary to protect herself from the wounds I inflicted. That she stood by me through all those years of heartache is remarkable.

Why did I stand by him? Some have believed it was because of my "great love" for him. While that sounds noble and wonderful, it just wasn't true. My love for Gerald had been attacked and wounded so many times over the years that it was in the process of dying. At this point, however, I believed that love would bloom afresh once the addictions were conquered and that we could again try to build our relationship. I felt it was just a matter of patience—he felt it was manifest indifference on my part. Throughout this time, my respect for him and his struggle never wavered, though there was reason to doubt the outcome. The fact that he kept trying, however, over and over again, to subject this part of his nature was reason enough for me to continue my support for him. But it was difficult to know how to do so.

After eight children and twenty years of ups and downs, we were both discouraged. We took what I thought was the easy way, avoiding conflict by living increasingly separate lives. Sadly, we were both learning to accept a hollow, empty relationship. It wasn't that we didn't care about each other, but I gave up hope that we would ever be happy together and we allowed ourselves to simply coexist, becoming increasingly indifferent and careless about the marriage. As the emptiness increased, LoAnne retreated into her relationship with the children and I retreated into work and addiction, allowing myself to become totally isolated from the family.[1]

---

1 As the First Presidency warned in the Family Proclamation, "husband and wife have a solemn responsibility to love and care for each other." There will always be trouble ahead when a couple substitutes anything for the importance of their relationship. In the March 2000 *Ensign*, Charles B. Beckert wrote a very helpful article about the very kind of life we were living at that time. It is called "The Pitfalls of Parallel Marriage." "If they're not careful," he warned, "couples sometimes end up living separate lives in the same home" (See pp. 22-25).

2. FINANCIAL STRESS

Before I committed the adultery that led to my excommunication, we were deeply in debt and in desperate need of additional income. Providing the necessities for eight children and meeting all the expenses with only one wage earner was a difficult challenge in the 1970s and I am sure it would be even harder today.[2] It seemed that no matter how many hours I worked, no matter what I did, I could never get ahead of the bills or keep our debt from growing. I was attempting to earn our living by total commission on sales of insurance and by preparing income tax returns (manually, in those days) for more than two hundred clients. Not having a steady, dependable income is scary under the best of circumstances, but facing that uncertainty with a large family depending on you is very stressful. There were many times that we had less than ten dollars in our checking account, with no commissions yet earned or on the way! But we always paid our tithing and somehow, the Lord always provided.

With continually rising expenses, the only answer I could see was to put more hours into wage-earning. Figuring I could schedule most of my tax appointments in the evenings, I accepted a full-time job doing physical labor, which was exhausting work six days a week. The only way to do that and to meet the demands of my tax clients during the income tax season was to begin the paperwork around 4:00 A.M. each morning. I didn't mind getting up so early, but in order to process the tax returns, which I did in the evening, my day never ended before midnight. The inevitable result of this nineteen to twenty hour schedule was utter physical and mental exhaustion.

As a result, I began to brood and to focus my thoughts on our problems instead of trusting the Lord to provide a way, as He always does when we are striving to live righteously. "And behold, all that he requires of you is to keep his commandments; and he has promised you that if ye would keep his commandments ye should prosper in the land; and he never doth vary from that which he hath said; therefore, if ye do keep his commandments he doth bless you and prosper you"

---

2 As today's culture grows more complex and expensive, it becomes increasingly difficult to support a family on one income. We know that sometimes it seems impossible to keep the mother in the home to nurture the children full-time. But even today, with proper education, career and budget management, it can be done if both parents are united and determined to find a way in cooperation with the Lord.

(Mosiah 2:22). The more I brooded over our empty marriage and other tribulations, the more the financial burden of supporting all those kids felt like a boulder to which I was chained.

One of the most important things I have learned, from my own experience as well as from others who have shared theirs with me, is that whatever holds or dominates the focus of your attention is going to hold and dominate you—your *feelings*, your *thoughts* and ultimately, your *choices*. This is especially true when you feel trapped in difficult circumstances that you do not seem to have the power to change. A person can endure almost any hardship when he knows that God understands what he is going through and that He cares and is support-ing him. But when your life is devoid of gratitude, when you see nothing but negativity and frustration, you are ripe for Satan's sly suggestions for what *appears* to be an easier way, but which always leads to greater problems.

By misdirecting the focus of my attention, I lost all appreciation for my blessings. Thus, instead of rejoicing in my role as a father and husband, instead of focusing on what special children we had been blessed with, instead of seeing the interesting personalities they had and how I could invest time in developing their potential, my family felt like a ball and chain around my neck. I am ashamed to admit that I felt more like a slave than a father or husband. Having chosen to ignore the laws of physical and mental health, and to overwork my body and mind to the breaking point, it is no wonder that I was disillusioned and unable to focus on anything but the negatives. Whenever we demand more of ourselves than is wise, we become extremely vulnerable to Satan's plan of escape from the pressures. Perhaps this is why the Lord counseled, "Do not run faster or labor more than you have strength and means provided . . . but be diligent unto the end" (D&C 10:4). In my Satanically twisted thinking, it seemed like I owed it to myself to find another life. I know now how selfish that was, but at the time, it seemed like I should have something for myself—even if it was only a few hours of loneliness in an apartment, unfettered by anyone else's needs.

I know now that gratitude opens the door to divine fellowship. The spiritual formula is this: the more we feel and express our grati-tude, the closer God will feel; and the less grateful we are, the further away He will seem. Thus Amulek taught that we should "live in thanks-giving *daily*, for the many mercies and blessings which he doth bestow upon [us]" (Alma 34:38). Elder Neal A. Maxwell warned, "Ingratitude reflects the intellectual dishonesty of those who can enumerate their grievances but cannot count their blessings" (*Notwithstanding My Weaknesses*, Salt Lake City, Utah, Deseret Book, 1981, p. 53). That was my experience. I have also learned that if there is any one thing Satan knows how to use as a lever with our ingratitude, it is *resentment*. I will show how he used my feelings as weapons against me.

In spite of the financial hardships we endured, I am so thankful now, that for most of our child-raising years, LoAnne was able to stay home with the children. Because of her devoted mothering, we now have nine children who are faithful and devoted to the gospel, men and women who love the Lord and are serving and helping to build the kingdom—this in spite of the poor example I was to them. They love our grandchildren (thirty at the time of this writing) and are raising them to love and serve the Lord as well. It is a priceless treasure worth all the hardship of that time!

3. SURRENDERING TO ADDICTION

After sincerely fighting the addictions for over twenty years, I had finally reached the point in my struggle that many addicts reach if they are not able to get help in their recovery: I gave up the struggle and surrendered to them. I reached the point where I got so tired of fighting the cycles that it seemed easier to just give in and suffer the guilt than to face the ever-repeating failure. It was a point where I justified my sin because it kept me going and I feared that without it, my whole life would crash. I did not choose this surrender because I preferred the sin. I hated it, but I was exhausted and just didn't have the time, energy, or will to fight it anymore. I didn't go looking for sin, but when the compulsions came, I just gave in so I could get on with what was left of my life. It seemed the only way to keep going. As Howard W. Hunter warned:

> There are times in our struggle with the adversities of mortality when we become weary, weakened, and susceptible to the temptations that seem to be placed in our pathways. Such a time is always the tempter's moment—when we are emotionally or physically spent, when we are weary, vulnerable, and least prepared to resist the insidious suggestions he makes [*Ensign*, Nov. 1976, p. 17].

As I retreated into my own world of fantasy and filth, I tried to avoid contact with everyone. My marriage got worse as I got worse.

Everything got worse. My work suffered and my family suffered. Because of this surrender, I felt even more hollow and hypocritical than I ever had before. I hated what I had become and loathed what I was doing, yet I returned to it again and again because I was just too tired to fight it any longer. I was beyond caring about myself or others. I was looking for *escapes* instead of *solutions*. I allowed feeling good in the present moment to become more important to me than making sure I was going to be right for eternity. Instead of supposing that I had failed in life, I believed Satan's lie that I was a failure. There is a big difference.

4. DROPPING OUT

As tax season progressed, I accumulated so much paperwork from the manually prepared tax returns that I could not keep up with it. (This was long before the days of computer-generated returns.) So, when the nineteen-hour days proved insufficient, I made the next major error. I resigned from my church assignments and stopped attending meetings so that I could use Sundays as a "catch up" day. It was the first—and only—time in my life that I deliberately chose to miss the Sunday meetings and it set a terrible example for our children. I assured them it was "just until tax season was over," but our teachings had been too strong for them to accept my flawed decision, even on a temporary basis. They were after me every Sunday. "Why aren't you coming with us, Dad? Please change your mind and come this time."

I could not stand the children's continual reminders of my deteriorating spiritual condition. My conscience was already hurting from all the compromises I had made, plus having surrendered to the addictions. I was in a state of agitated desperation, both financially and spiritually. So finally, instead of repenting, I screamed at my wife: "You get those kids off my back or I am leaving home!" Needless to say, that attitude from the husband, father, and priesthood holder only increased the tension in our family structure. The burden to resolve the tension fell, as usual, on my wife.

I chose the next day in family home evening to talk to the children. I knew Gerald would be gone doing taxes, and I hoped a frank discussion with the children would solve the problem. I tried to present the situation in such a way that they would feel compassionate and understanding of the pressure their father was under, but at the same time, I wanted them to know that his thinking was distorted and his decision to work on Sundays was a mistake. I wanted them to know that everyone must choose for themselves, and that when a person chooses wrongly, he must still be respected and loved and not judged.

It was a difficult task. I thought the children were accepting it reasonably well, however, until our twelve-year-old daughter realized what I was actually saying. Putting her face into her hands, she burst into tears, sobbing as though his soul was lost. They were all heartbroken over his decision.

I, too, was heartbroken about it. Always before I had been able to see that he was still trying to overcome these uncontrollable forces in his life, that his testimony was strong and that he cared about eternity. This was different. For the first time I was faced with the possibility that his choices would lead him away from the family and out of the Church. He seemed to be cutting himself off from everything that was important. I desperately wanted him to remember all he stood for, believed in and loved. However, he was too stressed out and exhausted to think straight, and in spite of my pleadings, he would not slow down, feeling he could not. He had no more trust in the Lord because he felt he had so often abused the Lord's trust in him.

So I resolved to try to smooth his life at home insofar as possible, and prayed for tax season to come to a speedy end. I thought that then he would be able to slow down and would be able to see things more clearly. I hoped his perspective would right itself and we could get back to being a whole family unit. Again, patience seemed to be the answer.

Making those shortsighted decisions did not mean that eternity and exaltation didn't matter to me anymore. I still had a testimony that the gospel and the Church were true. (The evidence is far too compelling to ever doubt that.) It just seemed too hard for *me* to live. I was being pulled apart by the "run-away-from-it-all" emotions on the one hand, and the pull of loyalty and duty on the other. I was empty and drained and I just could not cope with it anymore. I did not then realize that this is the role of grace, to step into and better the life of one who is willing to do the right things, but feels so worn out and inadequate that they can no longer fulfill those righteous desires on their own.

> This grace is an enabling power that allows men and women to lay hold on eternal life and exaltation after they have expended their own best efforts [*LDS Bible Dictionary*, p. 697].

I am sorry for the unwise choices I made. If I had accepted the enabling grace of Christ, they would not have been made, for He never requires that we go through such burdens alone. I regret the extra burdens, which were the result of my poor choices, on my wife and children. How important it is to stay close to the Lord, the scriptures, the Holy Spirit and to stay active in Church so that we may guard against those very first erosions of resolve. As the Savior warned: "Pray always lest that wicked one have power in you, and remove you out of your place" (D&C 93:49). Satan used his power to remove me from my place in the Church. The lessons about to enter our lives would be painful for all of us, but thankfully they have taught us that when a person has no room for God or family, his life is too full of the wrong things, and he is walking blindfolded in quicksand. Satan now had me prepared and ready for the next crucial part of his diabolical plan.

CHAPTER FOUR

MOVING TOWARD EXCOMMUNICATION

I could see that Gerald's lapses were getting beyond his control but I did not know what to do to help him. Then, as he grew worse, he tried to make me believe that his problems were largely my fault. I got so weary of the accusations that I made up my mind to always acquiesce to his demands so that he would not have any reason to lay the blame for his stress or misconduct on me. In spite of that, our relationship grew increasingly empty, and how could it be otherwise when I felt I was merely an instrument to satisfy his craving, rather than the object of his love?

But never saying 'no' to him didn't help for very long. He soon found another reason to accuse me. He said he felt cheated because he always had to "ask" (he used the word "beg"). It became a common theme of our disagreements. I have since learned that blaming others for their deviant behavior is a typical tactic of most abusers and addicts. I know now he was subconsciously, yet fiercely, attempting to put the burden of his guilt on me. It must have been a horrible burden for him to bear.

As I spent all my emotional reserves on trying to survive economically, I retreated into my own miserable world, leaving my family on the outside. Once I allowed my circumstances and negative feelings to override my testimony, my conscience, my duties and life-long priorities, it was not long before I abandoned prayer and scripture reading—for the first time in my adult life. And then it wasn't long before the hollow emptiness which these actions generated within me led me to conclude that things might be easier if I left the family and struck out on my own. Satan knew I wasn't ready for a major decision like divorce. But again and again he whispered that I just needed to get away for a few months and think things out. The more I thought about it, the more I decided that I owed it to myself to escape this "slavery" and find a life of my own. What selfishness!

I knew it would hurt LoAnne to learn that I had decided to leave. I had no idea how to tell her, but she soon sensed the change in my attitude and insisted on a heart-to-heart talk. After all those years of lonely sacrifice and suffering, trying to hold the marriage together, she became furious when I expressed my feelings and absolutely refused to accept the idea that moving out was a solution. She said she was convinced that everything would work out if I would only commit to stay until May 15th, thereby giving me a month after tax season ended to recuperate and regain my perspective. Surely, she reasoned, if we pulled together, we could somehow make things work until then. I disagreed, feeling that the separation was inevitable and that prolonging it would only increase her pain when it finally came. But it seemed so important to her that I reluctantly agreed to wait. I was just too weary to protest any further. So I trudged on through the muddle of my confused emotions, still ignoring the family and the Church, just numbly doing what had to be done each day.

My decision to leave the marriage had nothing to do with increasing the opportunity for sin. I had no intention of running away to a life of sexual escapades. I just wanted an escape from the pain of failure in my life, and from our frustrating, and what I felt was an intolerable, marriage, without realizing how much of the emptiness was my own fault and within my power to correct. I was completely unaware of how carefully Satan had wrapped his chains about me. I had no idea how carefully he had prepared me to accept the opportunity he was about to arrange for me to become involved with someone who could temporarily ease my pain by filling my loneliness and making me feel needed.

One of the important things we have learned these past years is that Satan knows exactly how to customize his temptations to meet our individual wants and needs. As President Kimball taught, "Lucifer and his followers know the habits, weaknesses, and vulnerable spots of everyone and takes advantage of them to lead us to spiritual destruction" (*The Miracle of Forgiveness,* pp. 218-19). For example, Satan knew that my conscience would not allow me to go out looking for another woman as long as I was married, so he brought a lonely woman to me through a referral from one of my tax clients.

Elder ElRay L. Christiansen said, "Satan and his aides no doubt may know of our inclinations, our carnal tastes and desires . . ." (*The New Era,* July 1975, p. 49). Thus, because of my addiction to pornography, Satan knew the best way to attract me to another woman would be by her appearance, rather than by something valid like personality, character or values. (I already had those in my present wife, but failed to appreciate them.) It was no coincidence that this woman had the perfect appearance of my dreams—it simply demonstrates the power of Satan to know our vulnerabilities and provide the perfect temptation. As President David O. McKay said, "Your greatest weakness will be the point at which Satan will try to tempt you . . . and if you have made yourself weak, he will add to that weakness" (*Improvement Era*, July 1968, p. 3).

Looking back, I think my greatest weakness at that time was not sexual, but was the loneliness caused by my years of empty pornographic fantasies. I wanted to feel needed by someone, but I had long ago trained my wife in the necessity of emotional independence, of functioning almost alone in our marriage. Satan knew that, and knew that even though this woman would be appealing to me, there was no way I would open up and admit to myself or to her: "I need you and I'm willing to violate my temple and marriage covenants to get what I need." So, instead of tempting me to admit my need for another woman, he provided a woman that needed me! She was divorced because of severe physical abuse from her former husband. She was insecure and starving for affection. Emotionally, she was in worse shape than I was. Wow! She needed me. It felt wonderful.

> It is possible that Satan can at least determine our susceptibility to a particular temptation from our words and actions, which reveal our thoughts. As the Savior taught, a tree is known by its fruit (Luke 6:43-45). Satan can see our fruits as well as any person—and we can be certain that he'll be quick to take advantage of the weaknesses we exhibit [Lawrence R. Peterson, *Ensign*, July 1984, p. 31].

We both felt an attraction to each other. It was fun being with her to do the taxes. I even thought about asking for a date, but that was beyond what I could give myself permission to do. But the memory of how good it felt to be with her haunted me and eventually I called her and asked if she would go for a walk in a park and help me sort out the problems I was having in my marriage. (A seemingly innocent and safe first step.) She agreed, and it felt so good to understand and feel sorry for each other that we spent the afternoon together. Then we took the next step by going to a movie. After the movie she made it clear that she wanted me and suggested a motel. One would expect, with my sexual addictions, that I would have viewed this as an unparalleled opportunity to fulfill my sexual dreams. But I did not. I recoiled in fear. No way! Adultery was the farthest thing from my mind. I told her that I loved being with her, but I had taken sacred vows that I could not break. (It never occurred to me that I was already breaking them just by being alone with her!) I emphasized to her that the most we could ever have together would be friendship.

However, the illusion of escape from my pain, which I was finding with her, seemed to be the most important thing in the world. Feeling the excitement of this new relationship seemed to be worth any price to make it mine forever. Forever—now, there was the problem. I had not forgotten the penalty for breaking temple covenants and I knew that even if I made our relationship legal by first getting a divorce, a relationship with a nonmember of the Church could never be ours forever. No matter how wonderful our life might be together in this world, I knew that it would have to end when death parted us, especially if I withdrew from a temple marriage to make it happen. But I had closed my mind to eternal consequences. I was just too worn out and too tired to worry about the *future*. I couldn't care about tomorrow anymore. This *now* had become too urgent to let go.

How incredibly warped and deluded my thinking had become! How important it is to hearken to the Lord's counsel as we make choices, to "let the solemnities of eternity rest upon your minds" (D&C 43:34). I had failed in my first marriage, yet in my hungry delusion I actually thought that by simply changing partners, we could build a wonderful new life together. How cleverly Satan deceives us into believing that it is sudden love that we feel when all it really amounts to is a selfish lust for a seemingly easy escape. I thought I had been lucky to find a wonderful friend. I had no idea I was being carefully led and deceived by Satan, just as Nephi had described: "And he leadeth them by the neck with a flaxen cord, until he bindeth them with his strong cords forever" (2 Nephi 26:22).

Unknowingly, step by step and compromise by compromise, I had allowed Satan to wrap his chains about me and "lead me carefully" to the ultimate betrayal. "And others will he pacify, and lull them away into carnal security . . . and thus the devil cheateth their souls, *and leadeth them away carefully down to hell*" (2 Nephi 28:22). Eventually I did what I had solemnly promised my God and my wife that I would never do. I desecrated the most intimate privilege that God has shared with mankind by committing adultery. Only then did I discover, when it was too late, what a shoddy and cheap imitation the devil offers.

"Be aware and warned of the subtle workings of Satan, for . . . he is an expert on making things seem appealing and right, when actually they can bring about our moral destruction" (Delbert L. Stapely, *Ensign*, May 1975, p. 22). What an incredible paradox. The attraction of what I was now feeling with this woman was the very thing I could have and should have been giving and receiving in my marriage! Satan carefully tempted me to nurture this woman because she had been abused and abandoned by a cruel, uncaring husband. But look how warped my thinking had become, for I was in the very act of cruelly abusing my own wife by betraying and abandoning her![1]

One excommunicated person told me how surprised she was when, following her adultery, the room they were in suddenly filled with laughter. The veil was removed from her eyes and she saw dozens of evil spirits who had been watching and were now pointing at her in derision as they laughed and rejoiced at the fall of another of God's children. As for myself, I saw no evil spirits. I heard no laughter. I just felt sick inside. Instead of finding happiness, I felt overwhelmingly dirty and ashamed. Satan had lied to me. This wasn't happiness. I had been cheated. I felt sick at heart. The ecstatic "live-happily-ever-after" dream I thought I was starting now seemed empty and very far away. And even worse, what had now been done could never be undone. I had made my choice. I had broken my vows. I had deliberately followed Satan into the sin which is second only to murder (See Alma 39:5), believing that I could turn and walk out on forty years of family and church and testimony and find peace and happiness with a stranger. To my surprise, it wasn't worth it after all. I had read Alma's warning dozens of times, but never understood or believed it till now: "Do not suppose . . . that ye shall be restored from sin to happiness. Behold, I say unto you, wickedness never was happiness" (Alma 41:10).

How could I have been such a fool? I had not done this because I was swept away with passion. I had deliberately and intentionally

---

1 Incredibly, until we committed adultery, it did not feel evil or wicked to be with this woman. Nurturing and loving her seemed like a noble and caring thing to do. But as Elder Richard G. Scott warned, "Satan will use rationalization to destroy you. That is, he will twist something you know to be wrong so that it appears to be acceptable and thus progressively lead you to destruction" (*Ensign*, May 1991, p. 35).

walked away from all that is precious and sacred and desecrated it with a stranger, expecting the reward of happiness. How could I have been so blind as to think I could steal love from someone I barely knew, when I hadn't learned how to give it to the one who had loved me and stood with me through twenty years of loyal service and devotion? "To hell with everyone else," I had thought. And now I realized, too late, that it was "to hell with me," and it wasn't even going to wait for the Day of Judgment. The Day of Judgment was right now. My conscience would not be silent. After a lifetime of sexual sin, I thought I was an expert in feeling guilty, but those years of relentless guilt had been nothing compared to the feelings that tortured me now.

In spite of all those years of failure and the recent assumptions that I might as well give up, I now realized that the gospel was in me too deeply to just up and walk away from my family, from my testimony and from God. As unthinkable as it seemed, I knew that somehow I had to find a way to go back and build a successful life with LoAnne and the children. My eight children—children that I did not deserve! I sat alone on the motel bed and took their pictures out of my wallet. I looked at them one by one for a long time. I looked at my wife's picture—and then I wept.

CHAPTER FIVE

THE RESCUE BEGINS

Making the decision to end this two-week relationship and go back to my family was not easy. But saying good-bye to this woman was even harder. We had promised each other that we were going to build a wonderful new life together, and here I was telling her good-bye before it had scarcely begun. She was hurt and she was furious. She yelled, she screamed and she cried. So did I. After making sure that I knew what a despicable creature I was, she stormed out of the motel. I was sorry to hurt her so abruptly, and as she slammed the motel door, I sat there thinking how I had now messed up *three lives*: my own, my wife's, and now this girl's. Three lives, indeed! I had no idea how the painful effects of this evil would penetrate the hearts of my children, our parents, brothers and sisters on both sides of the family, as well as our friends in the Church. Perhaps one reason immorality is such a serious sin is the way that it spreads out from the offenders, like ripples on a pond, to affect so many other lives.

To say that I felt confused and miserable as I sat there alone is completely inadequate. I had made the break and sent her away, but now I had to figure out how to go back to a wife I didn't know how to love, and how to go back to a church I didn't think I could live up to. My motives were based mainly on fear and guilt, but at least they were pointing me towards duty and repentance. As I sat there weeping, I thought I had made my choice by sending her home and that now I was on my way back. I thought my resolve was firm, but I was soon to discover how weak it really was. It wasn't very long before she came back to the motel, apologizing for all the names she had called me, and pleading for reconciliation. She insisted there was no way she was going to let me go out of her life. "We just have to stay together," she sobbed, "We need each other. We could make each other so happy. We deserve to finally get it right." Those flattering words were very tempting, but I stood firm and sent her away once again.

I was determined to resist her persuasions and get myself back on the correct course. Or so I thought. As I struggled through the next day I was continually haunted by her pleas, and even though I kept trying to tell myself I had made the right decision, I was being pulled apart by conflicting desires. I knew it was going to be very hard to go back to my duties and to succeed where I had failed for over twenty years, but somehow I had to try. Yet, throughout the day, I struggled with the urgent desire for her and the release from responsibility that she represented. By evening I was in real trouble. I wanted to go back to her so badly that I didn't see how I could possibly resist. All day I had been on the verge of phoning her. But, knowing that if I called her even once, or went to see her again, it would be making a decision that would change the rest of my life, I managed to resist the terrible pull of Satan's whispering temptation. I just had to preserve some hope of getting things right again with my family and the Lord.

After thinking all day about the terrible night before in the motel, I was so torn up inside that I just could not focus enough to keep my last appointment. So, after I called and canceled it, I went for a walk along an irrigation canal, hoping to think things through and figure out how to go home. Not a chance. I could not think. I just paced back and forth, the fear and uncertainty boiling uncontrollably inside me. I wanted desperately to pray for guidance, but that seemed unthinkable. I had ceased talking with my Heavenly Father months ago, when I had stopped going to church and had surrendered myself to the addictions. And now, after committing the unthinkable, how could I possibly expect Him to listen to me? I was ashamed to even think of involving Him in my despair. I didn't understand that Heavenly Father is a loving, merciful, caring and attentive Father. I didn't know of His anxious desire to help me to be obedient to His laws and commandments.[1]

Prayer might have come a lot easier for me had I remembered Lehi's testimony that "because thou art merciful, thou wilt not suffer those who come unto thee that they shall perish" (1 Nephi 1:14).

---

1 This misconception is perhaps the most common barrier to spiritual progress that I have encountered in the hundreds of readers and friends that have shared their quests with me. I devoted an entire book to breaking the barriers that normally prevent us from recognizing, believing and experiencing His tender and forgiving love, patience, kindness, compassion. See Steven A. Cramer, *In The Arms of His Love.*

There have been many others who have expressed to me similar barriers to their prayers because they too were ashamed of evil, selfish or unworthy desires and habits. It seems to be one of Satan's most effective weapons to fill our minds with doubts such as, "*You are not worthy to pray. After all you have done, He would never listen to you.*" Or, "*God is much too busy to get involved in such a small matter. How dare you ask such a thing of Him?*" Perhaps the most tragic of all: "*Who do you think you are to bother God with such a request?*" The truth is that honest prayers never bother our Heavenly Father. The way we do bother Him is by avoiding prayer, or by going through the motions of prayer, but refusing to honestly and frankly discuss our desires, burdens, heartaches and problems. As Elder Jeffery R. Holland said:

> I can tell you this as a parent: as concerned as I would be if somewhere in their lives one of my children were seriously troubled or unhappy or disobedient, nevertheless I would be infinitely more devastated if I felt that at such a time that child could not trust me to help or thought his or her interest was unimportant to me or unsafe in my care. In that same spirit, I am convinced that none of us can appreciate how deeply it wounds the loving heart of the Savior of the world when he finds that his people do not feel confident in his care or secure in his hands or trust in his commandments [*Ensign*, Apr., 1998, p. 19].

If we wouldn't be ashamed to go to our medical doctor for help with a fever or a rash, why should we be ashamed to go to our Heavenly Father when we need spiritual help? It is Satan who wants us to delay our prayers until *after* we are feeling clean and worthy, because he knows that if we do not pray *in* our need, we will *remain* in our need. The medical doctor doesn't look down on us for coming to him with a problem. Rather, he is happy for the opportunity to help restore our health. He respects us for caring enough about our health to take the appropriate action. And in His divine perfection and love, the Lord is delighted when we trust Him enough to share our problems and deepest feelings. He is not only willing, but eager to receive us and make us new. "Behold, he sendeth an invitation unto all men, for the arms of mercy are extended towards them, and he saith: Repent, and I will receive you" (Alma 5:33). As I agonized on that canal bank, I wish I'd had the understanding and faith of this simple, but powerfully adequate prayer: "Have mercy upon me, O Lord, for I am in trouble" (Psalms 31:9).

As I continued pacing, my fear and sobbing kept growing until I could contain it no more. Involuntarily, without deciding to pray, or even giving myself permission, the wounded spirit within me suddenly burst forth with an expression of sorrow for what I had done. I told the Lord how sorry I was for giving in after all those years of struggle. I confessed my awareness of how unworthy I was to ask for His help. It broke my heart to confess to Him that even then, right during that prayer, my desire to go back to her was so strong that I didn't see how I could resist—unless He had some way of strengthening me. And then the most astonishing, unexpected thing happened.

The moment I finished that tormented plea for help, that very instant the Lord manifested His love to me. Instantly His voice was in my mind, so real that it was almost audible. I stood frozen in my tracks, astonished by what I was feeling and hearing. There was no stern rebuke, no harsh or condemning judgment. This was a time for healing, not punishment. His voice was kind and gentle, even soothing, reassuring me that I was not alone in this problem. His peace filled my entire being, erasing my fears and witnessing to me that I was still loved. Loved? Yes! Loved no less than before I had committed this terrible act. The message was as clear and unmistakable as if He had physically appeared before my eyes. It would have been impossible to doubt that He heard my prayer and, more importantly, that He had a plan for rescuing me—or more correctly, for rescuing our family. Again I wept, overwhelmed by this unexpected, loving response.

Because of this experience, I feel a close relationship to the woman who was taken in the very act of adultery and then dragged before Christ. Throwing her at his feet, the accusers demanded His judgment. If Christ were not a God of love, forgiveness and acceptance, we might have expected Him to join in the condemnation. But, instead of shaming her in the presence of others, He turned to her self-righteous accusers. "He that is without sin among you, let him first cast a stone at her," He challenged protectively. "And they which heard it, being convicted by their own conscience, went out one by one." When they were alone, with tender compassion and love, He said to her, "Woman, where are those thine accusers? Hath no man condemned thee? She said, No man, Lord. And Jesus said unto her, *Neither do I condemn thee*: go, and sin no more" (John 8:7-11). His concern was not for the woman's *sin*, but for her *soul*. "For God sent not his Son into the world to condemn the world; but that the world through him might be *saved,*" and "He that believeth on him is not condemned . . ." (John 3:17-18).

But there is always a price to be paid and, though Jesus Christ has paid it, there is still a price He requires of us. What He requires is true repentance. Just being ashamed or sorry for our sins is not enough. The way the Lord measures repentance is this: "By this ye may know if a man repenteth of his sins—behold, he will *confess* them and *forsake* them" (D&C 58:43). In regard to the "forsaking" part of that divine formula, President Spencer W. Kimball has advised that the only successful way to begin our repentance of infidelity is with a total and abrupt amputation from all contacts and associations that led us into the sin. While his advice may seem hard or cruel, it is not just the best way to forsake our sin, it is the only way. We simply cannot truly repent as long as we insist upon compromise.

> In abandoning sin one cannot merely wish for better conditions. He must make them. He must be certain not only that he has abandoned the sin, but that he has changed the situations surrounding the sins.
>
> He should avoid the places and conditions and circumstances where the sin occurred, for these could most readily breed it again. He must abandon the people with whom the sin was committed. He may not hate the persons involved but he must avoid them and everything associated with the sin.
>
> He must dispose of all letters, trinkets, and things which will remind him of the "old days" and the "old times." He must forget addresses, telephone numbers, people, places and situations from the sinful past, and build a new life.
>
> He must eliminate anything which would stir the old memories. [*The Miracle of Forgiveness,* Salt Lake City, Utah: Bookcraft, Inc., 1969, p. 171-172].

Although my resolve was very weak and hesitant, I had begun the "forsaking" part back at the motel. But next must come the confession part and I was not prepared for that. This is where Satan snares many sincere and determined repenters. He has endless schemes of rationalization to help us live a double life of hypocrisy, pretending to repent while we continue to cling to our sin—or to at least hide it by avoiding confession. After exhausting his schemes to keep us ensnared in our sins, he finally says, in effect, "*Alright, go ahead and give it up if you must, but there is no need to humiliate yourself by confessing this before you repent and put it behind you. It would be better to wait until some time has passed. Later, after you are all cleaned up, then you can make it known if you must, but for now, your life will be better if you keep this to yourself."* I heard him and believed it. That was my plan! The devil knows that even if we do successfully abandon the sin, we can never find peace and forgiveness until we confess to the ones we have offended, to our bishop and to the Lord. Trying to repent without confession is Satan's fatal, going-only-part-of-the-way trap.

But now came the Lord's challenge. Now came the test on which hinged any future help from above. "*Gerald,*" He said, "*Are your sobbings to me from a repentant heart or from the misery of vacillation? If you mean what you say, you will go home right now and tell LoAnne everything.*" I was horrified at the pain that would cause her. "I can't do that," I cried in protest. Not realizing that I was falling into Satan's pseudo repentance—abandonment without confession—I said, "Let me go home and work on making things right with her first. Later, after we have made some progress in our marriage, after I'm doing better, after I've given her something worthwhile to hang onto, then I'll tell her." It sounded so *reasonable*—even kind and caring. But "my thoughts are not your thoughts, neither are your ways my ways, saith the Lord" (Isaiah 55:8).

"*You must go and tell her now,*" the wise command repeated. "*It is the only way.*" Again I bargained. "But I can't do it now. It would be so cruel. It will crush her. Give me time to get strong; time to reduce her hurt." Thankfully, His answer was the same, over and over until I ran out of protests. It seemed almost physical as the Spirit nudged me back into the car and I headed for home—for home and for broken hearts, but eventually, for healing, for the divine rescue of a new birth, a new life of freedom, purity and joy!

CHAPTER SIX

CONFESSION

Going home that night, just moments after my divine encounter on that canal bank, and telling LoAnne what I had done—with no time for preparation or planning of words—was far more difficult and heart wrenching for me than later telling our children, my parents, the bishop or the disciplinary council that would be assembled to bring me to account. One can only imagine the agony that it caused her when I returned home with my confession. After all her years of loyalty and patience, after standing by me in spite of the pornographic cycles and my indifference to her and the children, after all that sacrifice, I had finally betrayed her in the worst way possible.

When I exacted the promise from Gerald that he wouldn't leave our family before May 15ᵗʰ, he gave it to me on condition that I would allow him to get away for a day or two if he felt he needed it. I agreed to his condition and then he told me he needed that time right now. So, according to our agreement, he got a motel room and stayed away Sunday, Monday and Tuesday nights. I was concerned about him, but never doubted that this time away from home was anything more than an attempt to deal with his confusion and stress.

I have wondered since why I didn't suspect something was going on. I remember confronting the idea of infidelity several years before when Gerald joined a bowling league. He had invested in a ball and shoes and went a couple of times a week to the bowling alley. I accompanied him on a few occasions, but not often, because of the children. I remember clearly an occasion when one of his teammates, attempting to tease me for being there "to check up on my husband," tried to worry me about what his activities were when I was not there. Supremely confident, I replied that I never worried about such things. I knew Gerald would never be unfaithful to me, and I said so. How his teammates, none of whom were members of the Church, hooted at that! But, perhaps a little smugly, I knew in my heart that we both had testimonies that a temple marriage is forever; and I knew that my husband, who loved me and loved his church, would never do anything to destroy it. Little did either of us realize then, that by his pornographic binges and developing addiction, his loyalties were slowly, but surely, being drawn away from me and from the Church.

Anytime a person views or uses pornography, he is dabbling in infidelity because adulterous relationships are formed in his mind, whether the new partner is real or fantasized, whether the act is overt or imagined. Eventually that disloyalty builds and grows until there is no real faithfulness left. Mental and emotional lust is almost as great an unfaithful act as physical adultery, and is surely a precursor to the greater sin.

On Wednesday morning he came home with the announcement that he'd made a decision and that he was ready to try again. He brought me a beautiful vase of flowers. I was sick and in quite a lot of pain so that cheered me considerably. Then he left to go to his tax appointments for the day.

When he returned late that evening he was highly agitated and couldn't seem to say what was on his mind. As he paced frantically around the bedroom I could not get him to tell me what was wrong. (Even then, I was so naïve that I had no clue of what he was about to confess.) Gerald finally lay down beside me on the bed. He began to cry softly, but soon was overcome with great, racking sobs, saying over and over, "I just can't do it! I just can't do it!"

I couldn't imagine what was wrong, but I tried to comfort him. Finally he calmed a bit and then he told me. He said he had fallen deeply and desperately in love with another woman, a tax client, and that he had been unfaithful to me. There is no human expression of emotion adequate enough to express the hurt feelings of horror and anger I experienced. I cried a little. I didn't scream or yell, I just hurt deep inside as he told me of his terrible struggle to decide whether to confess and come back or to stay with her. He asked me if I would take him back.

All my life I'd believed that if my husband were ever unfaithful to me, it would be such a serious breach that our marriage would end, and rightly so, I thought. I knew I'd never be able to make love to him again, and I felt divorce would be the only right answer. But on that horrible night as I considered what to do, all I could think was, "Heavenly Father still loves this man," and "We are commanded to forgive every man his trespasses."

At this point, I was hurting so badly that all I wanted to do was turn to God, who loved me, and to find a release from this pain in my heart. I realized, also, that I must do what God wanted me to do, for in only that way could I obtain peace. Heavenly Father blessed me with knowledge of what I must do. I had to be willing to forgive, first of all. And secondly, I knew that if Gerald was truly repentant and willing to pay the price, my duty was to stay with him.[1]

I asked Gerald if he was willing to come back all the way—into the Church and the family as well as to me. He said he was. I asked him to give me his word of honor that he would never see or communicate with the other woman in any way ever again. He seemed shocked with the request. He said he couldn't make that promise because he loved her, and it would be heartless to end all communication so immediately. I told him that he couldn't have it both ways. I was drawing a line and he had to choose. Our future hinged on that and on his willingness to pay the price of total repentance—which meant total commitment to our marriage, our children and the Church; and with no further indulgence in pornography.

Then I went downstairs to call the bishop to ask him for an appointment the first thing in the morning. He said he'd come by the house, and I told Gerald he had until then to decide. We parted then—he went upstairs and I stayed downstairs—to spend a long, lonely, sleepless night.

Though the night was fraught with fear and uncertainty, and I felt torn by conflicting emotions, I knew without doubt that Heavenly Father had heard my inward cries and had answered my prayer. And because I chose to follow His divine counsel which was spoken quietly in my mind, I received a peaceful assurance that I was loved, that God would be with me, and that He would help me through the trials to come. The deep, searing pain in my chest was gone, replaced by a sort of numbness. The physical relief I received was undeniable, and the spiritual fortification He gave me that night would see me through some very precarious times to come.

By morning Gerald had realized the wisdom of the commitment I was requesting of him and gave me his word never to see the other woman again and to talk to her by phone only once in order to inform her of the fact. He made his confession to the bishop. Events were set in motion that would change our lives forever.

I will be eternally grateful to LoAnne for her response to that night's painful horror. After so many years of mental and emotional infidelity, so many years of verbal and emotional abuse, and now this report of adultery, I had absolutely no right to claim or expect forgiveness or kindness. Yet, her great spirit was able to look beyond her pain toward "choosing the right." I do not remember a single moment's reprisal or revenge from that night or in the years to follow, though there would be many times that I deserved it.[2]

---

1 This was personal revelation to me and does not reflect the requirement of God for all wives in these cases. See more on this in Appendix A.

2 Learning how to forgive others and learning to accept God's forgiveness is discussed in p. 101-111 & 161-169 of *In The Arms of His Love*.

I stand in awe at the example of discipleship she manifested. Throughout this entire ordeal, her utmost desire was to be in harmony with the Lord's will for our family. She felt that whatever that meant, whether it was a divorce, or still further forgiveness, her duty was to find His will and then do it. How blessed I was to have such a noble wife. How blind I was to have ever been insensitive to her loyal support and love.

CHAPTER SEVEN

SATAN'S POWER

President Kimball emphasized that it is important to have "an awareness of the existence, the power, and the plans of Satan . . ." (As quoted by Elder ElRay L. Christiansen, *Ensign*, Nov. 1974, p. 24). So much of what happened to me could have been avoided had I known my enemy and how he affects our thought processes. I am certain that my thirty years of captivity could have been much shorter. But I did not understand; it was as though I was fighting those life and death circumstances blindfolded, unable to detect or defend against my enemy. It was years before my understanding grew beyond blaming only myself for making bad choices to recognizing the role Satan played in maneuvering me into those choices.

Many people feel that if they ignore the reality of the devil and avoid thinking of him, they will somehow be protected from his influence, but precisely the opposite is true. It is difficult, if not impossible, to conquer an enemy we do not recognize, understand or respect. President Benson counseled: "A study of Satan's methods can alert us to his seductions" (*Ensign*, July 1973, p. 8). And Jesus said that knowledge of gospel truths will make us free. (See John 8:32) On the other hand, ignorance of Satan and his powers can make us slaves, captives and prisoners of war, bound by the very chains of hell—as I was. The Lord warned through Isaiah, "My people are gone into captivity, because they have no knowledge . . ." (2 Nephi 15:13).

> They must be taught that Satan is real and that he will use all agencies at his disposal to tempt them to do wrong, to lead them astray, make them his captives, and keep them from the supreme happiness and exaltation they could otherwise enjoy [N. Eldon Tanner, *Ensign*, July 1973, p.8].

The less we believe in Satan, and the less we understand and recognize his "cunning devices," the more power he can exert over us (See

Alma 10:13). Elder Melvin J. Ballard said, "It is well to know the forces and the powers that are arrayed against us, and their purposes, that we may close ranks and fortify ourselves" (*The New Era*, Mar. 1984, p. 38). The following is an explanation of some of the techniques used by Satan to persuade people to heed his wicked suggestions and an account of how he applied those tricks to me.

Pre-eminent among all of Satan's powers is the ability which he and his demons have to place thoughts and suggestions in our minds by speaking to us secretly, without our conscious knowledge. Satan and his demons are still spirits, but without physical bodies. This enables them to speak directly to the spirits inside our bodies, without us even being consciously aware of the suggestions they make.[1] Joseph Fielding Smith, Jr. warned of the danger this ability can pose:

> We should be on guard always to resist Satan's advances. He has power to place thoughts in our minds and to whisper to us in unspoken impressions to entice us to satisfy our appetites or desires and in various other ways he plays upon our weaknesses and desires [*Answers To Gospel Questions*, comp. 5 Vols., Salt Lake City, Utah: Deseret Book Co., 1957-66, vol. 3:81].

"We are surrounded by demons, yea, we are encircled about by the angels of him who hath sought to destroy our souls" (Helaman 13:37). These demons follow us everywhere we go. They observe everything that goes on in our life, unceasingly, around the clock, twenty-four hours a day. They can observe our desires, our strengths, values and priorities. They also observe where we are weak and vulnerable. They use this knowledge to whisper temptation and discouragement to us (through our spirits) without us even being aware of it. "And behold, others he flattereth away and telleth them there is no hell; and he *saith* unto them: I am no devil, for there is none—and thus he whispereth in their ears, until he grasps them with his awful chains . . ." (2 Nephi 28:22). Ronald A. Dalley said, "There is not a person alive who has not, at some point in his life, had an inappropriate thought enter into his

---

1 Satan uses the same method of communicating with our spirits that the Lord and the Holy Ghost use. As Sister Ardeth G. Kapp said, "The Holy Ghost communicates with us through 'whisperings' just as Satan and other spirit beings do" (*Ensign*, Nov. 1990, p. 94). Mormon related the influence of the Spirit's "whisperings" in guiding him as he condensed the sacred records of centuries into the Book of Mormon we have today: "I do this for a wise purpose; for thus it whispereth me, according to the workings of the Spirit of the Lord which is in me" (The Words of Mormon 1:7).

mind, primarily because Satan has the power to put it there" (*The New Era*, Aug. 1984, p. 45).

> Thoughts originate from three sources—from within us, from the prompting of the Holy Spirit, and from the evil sources around us provided by Satan and his hosts as they "whisper in our ears." We must, therefore, learn to recognize the source of our thoughts and control them accordingly [Ronald A. Dalley, *The New Era*, Aug. 1984, p. 44].

We see an example of his deceptive, manipulative whisperings in the dishonest contribution made by Ananias and his wife, when Peter said: "Ananias, why hath Satan filled thine heart to lie to the Holy Ghost, and to keep back part of the price of the land?" (Acts 5:3) Similarly, when we have opportunities to serve others and to build the kingdom, Satan whispers suggestions to hold back our money, time and service, hoping we, too, will choose a more selfish way to use our resources. The lies and secret combinations which Gadianton used to manipulate society "were *put into the heart* of Gadianton by that same being who did entice our first parents to partake of the forbidden fruit . . ." (Helaman 6:26; also 27-29).

Satan and his demon tempters are masters at manipulating mortal thoughts and emotions through the vicious whisperings that they have perfected on billions of our predecessors. They know how to stimulate worry and doubt, hatred and fear, resentment and jealousy, stress, anger, lust, depression, feelings of emptiness, loneliness and frustration, etc. No such feelings come from above. These destructive nudges come from the influence of powerful demonic spirits who know how to whisper suggestions that trigger our self-defeating emotions and thought patterns and who then laugh and rejoice at our misery.[2] Another goal of Satan and his demons is to make us believe that we are bad; that we are worthless and hopeless; that God couldn't possibly love us the way we are. That is the way the devils design their whisperings. They will beat on us with every whispered lie, temptation and discouragement possible to distort our self-image and limit our relationship with God.

We know that God did not create any unimportant people, or "nobodies," as they are popularly called. We are all His divine offspring, designed and destined to become like Him. Jesus believed in us enough

---

2 For examples of the devil's laughter and pleasure in our sins and mistakes, see 3 Nephi 9:2; Moses 7:26; 5:21.

to leave His throne of glory to suffer and die for us, so why would we believe Satan's lies that we are worthless and unimportant even though we may have made some bad choices? Unfortunately, once Satan persuades us to *feel* like an unimportant nobody, he has prepared us to *act* like a nobody. Thus, another purpose of his "whisperings" is to *lead* us into self-defeating attitudes and behaviors, and then to *keep* us trapped in them once we are there.

Just as doctors implant electronic pacemakers to regulate the function of defective hearts, Satan tries to regulate our behavior by "whispering" lies, deception, discouragement and temptation in our ears in order to implant unworthy feelings, desires and values in our hearts. If we are not aware of this diabolical effort, and if we fail to protect ourselves against this dangerous influence, these evil suggestions will find their way into our minds and hearts, where we mistake them for our own thoughts, impressions and feelings. And when that happens, we can make some pretty stupid choices—as I did. That was how Satan manipulated me. It is how he tempts and manipulates everyone who is not aware that they are being manipulated.

Throughout the years of addiction that eventually led to my disciplinary church court, and for quite some time afterwards, I assumed my marriage problems and sordid habits were strictly the result of my own poor judgment and bad choices, never dreaming that I had been deceived and manipulated by Satan's cruel "whisperings." It was only after hundreds of other sufferers disclosed to me how they too had been deceived that I began to recognize the repeating and very predictable *patterns* of Satan's lies.[3] Only then did I discover that I had allowed myself to fall under the influence and illogic of the master deceiver. Once I came out of the spiritual stupor that had enabled me to do what I had done in breaking my marriage and temple covenants, I felt devastated by shame and guilt. And later, when I found out about Satan's "whisperings" and how I had been duped and manipulated, I felt really stupid.

---

3 The power of Satan and his demons to transfer manipulative suggestions and lies through our spirits into our conscious minds is discussed in Chapters 3, 4 and 5 of *Putting On The Armor of God.* Also in Chapter Nine of *In His Image.*

HOW HE WHISPERED TO ME

As that fateful tax season continued, I felt increasingly miserable and hopeless. I was desperate for an escape. Into this self-inflicted void came Satan, gleefully filling my mind with his whispered lies. He had a strategic, progressive plan to use against me. (He has one for every-one.) First, he began by reminding me of all my moral failures. Surrounding me with unseen demons who could whisper in my ears twenty-four hours a day (See Helaman 13:37; 2 Nephi 28:22), he made sure I was constantly reminded of how hard I had tried to overcome pornography and masturbation through my twenty-eight years of struggle. Day after day he reminded me of all the various things I had tried, and of course, that in none of them had I been successful. As I reviewed my life, these reminders were very discouraging—especially because I knew the tremendous effort I had expended, and because I had no idea or hope of how I could make the future any better.

Robbing us of hope with feelings of discouragement is one of Satan's powerful weapons for breaking our will and persuading us to compromise or to give up the struggle. President Ezra Taft Benson said: "As the show-down between good and evil approaches with its accompanying trials and tribulations Satan is increasingly striving to overcome the Saints with despair, discouragement, despondency, and depression" ("Do Not Despair," *Ensign*, Oct. 1986, p. 2).

One of Satan's major goals is to destroy families. Included in the next phase of the demons' whisperings were constant reminders of how lonely I felt. They taunted me with continual thoughts of how unlikely it was that I would ever find happiness with "this wife." They whispered suggestions of resentment towards her. Satan and his demons whispered that I deserved a better companion because she never had and never would fulfill my illusionary, pornographic "dream girl" fantasy images (as if that was my right), nor give me the companion-ship and happiness that I desired. (Of course they never mentioned my responsibility in our relationship problems.) I believe that most people today would recognize those whisperings that attacked my confidence, self-worth and marriage as far too familiar echoes from their own thoughts.

Satan's third line of attack was genuinely custom-made for my sit-uation. It was this part of his strategy that proved to be the greatest influence in my final descent. The demons directed my thoughts to the fact that just as there will be three degrees of glory and three different types of people in the next life, there are also three kinds of people in the Church right now: celestial, terrestrial, and telestial. And of course this is true.[4]

Christ is continually inviting us to rise above the natural man, to become celestial people by striving for the attainment of His image and likeness in our characters and personalities. Paul expressed this stunning invitation as a *process* by which we keep learning, growing and progressing until, through the power of Christ's atonement and grace, we come "unto the measure of the stature of the fulness of Christ" (Ephesians 4:13). What an incredible opportunity! But we have the right to choose not to become like Christ. The deceptive and destructive part of Satan's scheme is in trying to persuade us to lower our goals, to "face reality" and just to "be ourselves," which always means to be our *lesser selves*, our fallen selves.

Therefore, as the demons reminded me of my lifetime of failure, both in my morals and my marriage, they also whispered that I was never going to become a celestial person. Over and over they asked when I was going to face up to this reality and quit torturing myself. Why was I so proud? Why was I making my life so miserable by trying to be more than I was capable of being? To make it easier to lower my sights, they suggested that giving up on attaining the celestial kingdom wasn't like I was admitting failure or choosing something degrading. All it meant was that I would finally admit that most of me was pretty good, but I just wasn't celestial material. And that was okay, they soothed, because I could still do good and be of service in one of the lower kingdoms. Surely God must need people there too, or He wouldn't have created the lesser kingdoms.

As I pondered these suggestions, I had no idea that these new thoughts were coming from satanic enemies who were bent on my destruction. I thought that I was coming to see myself more realistically. I actually believed these conclusions were out of my own reasoning. Yet, even though these ideas seemed to make sense, there was a small whisper somewhere deep inside that told me there was something wrong with that logic. (I didn't then understand that through the

---

4 Humanity is not divided into these three categories because we are somehow predestined or limited by our creation, but because of the kind of people we make of ourselves as we make choices and determine what is important or not important to us. (See D&C 88: 19-24)

power of Christ, every person who is *willing* and *chooses* to attain exaltation may be guided and enabled to do so through Christ. I now know with certainty that the gospel plan is for every child of God; not only for "superstars," but for even the weakest among us.) So, there I was, almost convinced by Satan's deception, but wavering.

The demons completed their deception by reminding me that God created this mortal life for us so that we could experience greater joy (2 Nephi 2:25)—a commandment, they whispered, that I was not obeying. "*God wants to make you happy,*" they taunted, "*but you won't let him.*" (The demons are expert at quoting and twisting scripture.) "*And by the way,*" they reminded, "*the burden of all those kids and bills is ruining your life and robbing you of the joy you deserve and that God wants you to have.*" Wasn't it about time I gave up the slavery of supporting my family and started getting some of that joy for a change? They lied that if I would just give in and be my "real self," *I would still inherit all the joy I was capable of experiencing,* while eliminating the pain and frustration of trying to force perfection on myself. That is a very persuasive argument to someone who has lost his perspective and wants to find an escape or an easier way. As President Kimball warned:

> Lucifer, in his diabolical scheming deceives the unwary and uses every tool at his command. He will use his logic to confuse and his rationalization to destroy. He will shade meanings, open doors an inch at a time, and lead from purest white through all the shades of gray to the darkest black [*Ensign*, Nov. 1980, p.94].

I was in such a state of physical exhaustion, emotional agitation and spiritual distress, that my self-image was shattered. I felt that in addition to being an economic failure because of our growing debt and inadequate provision for my family, I was also a failure as a husband, a failure as a father and most certainly, a failure as a man of morals. Indeed, I felt that I was a total failure. In my desperate longing for relief, I was ripe to believe anything that would make life seem easier. Through the persuasive power of their whispered lies, the devils convinced me that if I would just trade the celestial potential of exaltation (which God has given each of us) for Satan's degraded picture of me, I wouldn't have to try so hard and I would then feel better. When I feebly tried to counter their whisperings with my duty to endure to the end and never give up, the devils called me stupid and prideful. They challenged me to be realistic for once in my life. Didn't the last twenty-eight years of failure prove that I would be much more comfortable and, therefore, much happier in one of the lower kingdoms? Over the weeks, as the tax season progressed, these demanding, unceasing thoughts pounded in my mind. Eventually, the persistent whisperings began to influence my decisions. I began to accept this treacherous path that Satan was suggesting. He grew more and more bold until he was shouting at me every waking moment that giving up and leaving home was the only way to real peace. It all seemed to make sense and I was agreeing with him without realizing that I had been deceived. "And others will he pacify . . . and thus the devil cheateth their souls, *and leadeth them away carefully down to hell*" (2 Nephi 28:22).

I am embarrassed to disclose that I fell for such obvious deceptions. I suppose it seems amazing that a person could actually believe such lies, but it can happen to anyone who forfeits their claim upon the Holy Ghost and the discernment between truth and error which He gives to those who live worthy of His guidance.

SATAN'S POWER IS LIMITED

Some well-meaning people have tried to dissuade me from sharing what I have learned about Satan's strategies. They believe that talking about them only gives him greater power over us. I respect that opinion, and I admit that it is both frightening and offensive to learn that Satan can manipulate our thoughts and feelings without our knowledge or consent. But the truth is that many of the prophets have emphasized his power to do this. It is part of the spiritual war which continues from the premortal world, part of the "opposition in all things" to which we each agreed before we came here. And that is one reason, they say, that it is so important to study the scriptures daily and to keep ourselves armed and in tune with the Holy Spirit.

While the ability of Satan's army to surround us and whisper lies, distortions and discouragement is alarming and cause for serious caution, we should rejoice in the knowledge that Satan can never force us to listen or to obey his lies. He can have no more power over our minds or hearts than we allow. Through the influence of the Holy Ghost, we can discern and reject all Satan's evil suggestions. Lawrence R. Peterson, Jr. explained: "As a being of spirit, he works in the realm of spirit, counterbalanced by the Spirit of God. In this way, free agency is preserved, giving us a choice between good and evil. As Lehi taught, 'Man could not act for himself save it should be that he was enticed by the one or the other' (2 Nephi 2:16)."

If Satan entices us to do evil so the Holy Spirit "entices" us to virtue (See Mosiah 3:19). *Free agency demands that neither the Holy Spirit nor the evil spirit have power to control the person against his will* [*Ensign*, July 1984, p. 31].

Learning to ignore Satan's whisperings so that we can listen to the whispering of the Holy Spirit is very much like tuning a radio. Though the air is filled with radio waves broadcasting every conceivable type of program, a radio can play only one station at a time. And so it is spiritually: either we tune in to the Lord's frequency or to Satan's "whisperings." Both sides are "broadcasting" urgent messages to influence our thoughts, feelings and choices. "I will tell you [whisper] in your mind and in your heart, by the Holy Ghost, which shall come upon you and which shall dwell in your heart" (D&C 8:2). Neither side can compel us to listen to the messages they send. We have both the agency and the responsibility to choose which whispered signals we allow ourselves to focus upon. As Boyd K. Packer stated, this we *can* do and this we *must* do:

> All inspiration does not come from God (See D&C 46:7). The evil one has the power to tap into those channels of revelation and send conflicting signals which can mislead and confuse us. There are promptings from evil sources which are so carefully counterfeited as to deceive even the very elect (See Matthew 24:4). Nevertheless, we can learn to discern these spirits [*Ensign*, Nov. 1989, p. 14].

Knowing the determination of Satan's demons to lead us with negative thoughts and feelings into damaging behavior patterns can free us to discern their source and then choose to listen to the loving inspiration and encouragement that our Heavenly Father and his angels are also whispering. Learning to recognize and then shut out the manipulations of Satan's whisperings can prepare us to receive the promptings of the Holy Ghost.

Satan most certainly took advantage of his knowledge about my weaknesses and difficult circumstances. His deceptions were brilliant, manipulative and tailor-made. But he could not have "led me carefully down to hell" as he did unless I had made it possible by my lack of spirituality and ignorance of his tactics. My blindfold is now gone and yours should be, too.

CHAPTER EIGHT

EXCOMMUNICATION

Behold, happy is the man whom God corrected: therefore
despise not thou the chastening of the Almighty (Job 5:17).

In the April 1972 General Conference, Elder Robert L. Simpson
was asked to give the members of the Church an explanation of
Church discipline, as manifest in the court procedures now known as
disciplinary councils. He opened this subject by saying, "May I take a
few moments at this session of our conference to discuss what I believe
is perhaps *the most misunderstood meeting of all the meetings* that convene
in the church. I refer to the bishop's court" (Ensign, July 1972, p. 48).

The morning after I confessed to my wife, our bishop came to our
home to comfort her and provide counsel about the crisis my sin had
caused. After his talk with her, I made my initial confession to him.
Because of my pride and fear, it was more of an "admission" than a
humble confession. When our bishop reported to the stake president
what I, a former bishop, had done, he called back to tell us they would
be scheduling a high council disciplinary court to decide whether or
not my membership would be removed. I was stunned, even offended
by this unexpected news. It is an illustration of what the scriptures
mean when they talk about Satan *raging* "in the hearts of the children
of men" to "stir them up to anger against that which is good" (see 2
Nephi 28:20). Although I did not recognize his influence at that time,
I can now see clearly how Satan and his demons came rushing to take
advantage of that opportunity to confuse me and poison my attitude.

Having no idea that a church disciplinary action was going to be
so beneficial to me—a bitter but helpful procedure prescribed by a loving Heavenly Father to help me heal spiritually—I quickly became a
victim to the raging whispers of Satan's demon tempters. "*Wait a
minute*," they shouted in my ears. "*What right do they have to drag you into*

a church court? What a slap in the face! You broke off that silly affair after only knowing her for two weeks! And then you came back to make things right voluntarily. You confessed voluntarily. You don't need a disciplinary council to turn you around. You already promised to repent. And now they are going to haul you into a church court and try you for your membership!" The worst whisper of all was this one: *"If they are going to excommunicate you anyhow, you might as well go back to the other woman and be happy."* This suggestion would prove to haunt me, even after the court.

The manipulative whisperings of my enemy, calculated to make our already precarious situation even worse, quickly nudged me into an attitude of resentment and rebellion. The more I thought about the embarrassment and humiliation I expected a disciplinary action to cause, the more indignant I grew. "Well," I thought, "if that is the way they want to treat someone who voluntarily leaves an opportunity to be happy, who voluntarily comes back to do his duty, then I just won't even go to their silly court. I'll show them!"

These were the subtle, whispered ideas and suggestions of Satan and his minions. I bought it because I was more possessed of pride than humility. I wanted to run and hide without having to face my church leaders with what I had done. This experience would eventually teach me that Christ is the only "way out" of our difficulties and that our Heavenly Father loves us too much to leave us wallowing in our defeat, undisciplined and uncorrected, even if it requires the temporary spiritual amputation of an excommunication to help us recover. No matter how deeply in trouble a person might be, Christ already has a way and a plan prepared for his rescue, just as He had for me (See 1 Nephi 10:18).

MY ATTITUDE CHANGES

As I continued to struggle with those rebellious feelings, our bishop gave me a copy of the previously mentioned talk on church courts by Elder Robert L. Simpson, as found in the July, 1972 Ensign, pages 48 and 49. Reading that talk softened my attitude. During the weeks we waited for the court to convene, I also reread President Kimball's book, *The Miracle of Forgiveness*. I had read it several years before, but at that time it had no significant impact on me. But now I read it from the perspective of one in desperate need of hope. It was like clear, pure water to my aching thirst. Both of these sources convinced me that I had done something far worse than I had realized. As I began to see my sins from God's perspective, I began to realize how horribly I had offended Him by violating my covenants. As my spirit was humbled during those waiting weeks, I could see more clearly the position of the Church, which I had also desecrated by my unworthy actions.

I have known people who grew bitter and blamed priesthood leaders for the actions taken by their Church disciplinary councils. Unquestionably, everything associated with such councils is painful and difficult, both to administer and to receive. They fail to understand that it was God, not man, who revealed the judicial system of our Church government. Heavenly Father and Jesus are perfect; everything they do and everything they reveal to priesthood leaders is also perfect, or at least, as close to perfection as we, in our mortal weaknesses, can administrate.

When the brother of Jared asked the Lord to illuminate sixteen stones so that they might have light inside their ships, he taught an important principle that relates to many things in our lives, including disciplinary councils. He said, "I know, O Lord, that thou hast all power, and can do whatsoever thou wilt for the benefit of man . . ." (Ether 3:4). To me this means that if there were a better way to reclaim a person who has seriously sinned than disfellowshipment or excommunication, the Lord not only *could*, but He *would* do it differently. Thankfully, I was able to use those several waiting weeks before my council to overcome all the nasty, bitter feelings of resentment and petty embarrassment that Satan had whispered to me. I began to look forward to the council. I felt certain that once the brethren heard my full story, I would most certainly be excommunicated, but amazingly, I no longer viewed it as a slap in the face or as some kind of punishment. I felt that if that was what I needed to be totally square with the Church and the Lord, then it was not something to *dread*, but something to *look forward to*. Though I certainly did not fully understand it at that time, I had come to sense that somehow, in the Lord's wisdom, this would not be the *end* for me, but a new *beginning*, and I was anxious for it.

OUR COURT EXPERIENCE

My experience validates all I have said in this chapter and in Appendix B. The meeting was held in the high council room at the stake center. All twelve high councilors were there, along with the stake presidency and one stake clerk—sixteen brethren with whom I had served in various positions.

I could tell the high councilors had not been told in advance who was to be tried, because as LoAnne and I entered the room where they awaited us, I could see the shock and pain in their faces. After that first glance, they politely avoided looking directly at me, a consideration that I certainly appreciated. It was obvious during the entire procedure that it was an extremely painful experience for them, something that no priesthood bearer would enjoy, but rather, would prefer to avoid. But it was also something they would do to the best of their ability because it was part of their duty, required by the Lord who now needed their help in the recovery of a sheep who had gone astray. I am grateful those priesthood brethren loved me enough to do their duty.

The proceedings were simple. First, we all knelt around the table for a most beautiful and touching prayer, pleading for the Lord's Spirit to guide the affairs of the council. The stake president then explained the charges against me. He asked me if they were true and I acknowledged that they were. He gave our bishop the opportunity to comment first, and then invited LoAnne to express her feelings.

I have very little memory of what I said on that occasion. I do remember that it was a most difficult and dreadful event for me. I commented to them that it would be easier to face Gerald's death than to deal with this shameful situation in our lives. I now realize that, while death seemed more honorable to me then, the overcoming of sin and Satan carry much more honor than the escape of death. Nevertheless, I expressed my confidence in the men there assembled and bore my testimony of faith that they would act in accordance with the Lord's will. I pledged to abide by their decision—but in light of Gerald's humility and honesty, I really did not believe it would involve excommunication.

Then I was told that I could say whatever I wanted in regard to this transgression, as well as any others that I felt were pertinent to the judgment and decision of the council. When we are tried for a crime in a regular court of justice, the usual legal advice is to deny everything and admit nothing, placing the full burden of proof on the prosecutors. By contrast, when we break God's commandments, the best advice is full confession, which leads to forgiveness, healing, and the transfer of our debt to the Atonement of Jesus Christ.

Confession is a necessary requirement for complete forgiveness. It is an indication of true "godly sorrow." It is part of the cleansing process. Starting anew requires a clean page in the diary of our conscience [J. Richard Clarke, *The New Era*, Nov. 1980, p. 4].

Feeling nothing but love and sorrow from the members of the council made it easy for me to be open and honest. I confessed my adultery as well as the struggles I had endured since I was a youth. I confessed my cycles of addiction to masturbation and pornography, as well as my efforts to repent and free myself of those awful taskmasters. As I began my confession, I felt a very heavy burden lifting from me. Instead of the confession *increasing* my pain, each confessed sin seemed to *reduce* the weight of my burden. When I was done they asked if there was anything else that I should mention. What a great relief it was to be able to say, "No, that was everything." I felt as though an enormous weight had been lifted from my shoulders.

> It is confession that *starts* the process of forgiving. It is a healthy, healing thing to drop all evasions and say that you have failed, sinned, blundered, hurt someone, disappointed yourself. This is the place to start. Admit it. All else comes later. Until you get over this hurdle, you have not started the race. Until you open this door, the fresh air and sunshine that awaits you will be locked out [Don Baker, *Forgiving Yourself*, Portland, Oregon: Multnomah Press, 1985, p. 23].

After my confession the members of the council questioned me to gain a clearer understanding of my sin and my heart. Again I was shown the utmost respect and courtesy. As dismayed as these brethren must have been about what I had done, they never showed the slightest trace of criticism or condemnation. Instead, their attitude toward me was a clear expression of compassion and sorrow for what I had suffered and for the coming consequences. Truly, it was "a court of love." LoAnne and I were then dismissed to wait in another room with our bishop while they deliberated their decision. I was amazed that it took them almost an hour to discuss the case and pray about alternatives. It was obvious to me that they did not jump to a conclusion nor take their duty lightly.

After what seemed an eternity of waiting, we were invited back and the decision of excommunication was announced to us. The stake president explained the terms and restrictions of their decision. I was no longer a member of God's church. My priesthood was removed. I must immediately remove my temple garments and live without their protection or their reminder of temple covenants and promises— which I had broken. Furthermore, I realized, not only was I outside the *Church*, but also outside my *family*, for the sealing ordinances to my wife and children were dissolved. We were now married only until parted by death. Like any nonmember, I would still be allowed to attend public church meetings, but unlike them, I would not be allowed to participate in class. I could not pray aloud in church, bear my testimony or even raise my hand to sustain callings and releases. I would be denied the sacrament. The list of restrictions seemed to go on and on.

After the council closed with prayer, the brethren immediately expressed their love and support for me. And in the coming years, every time I saw one of these men, they were always eager to shake hands with me and give me an eye-to-eye expression of warm love and support. I came away from that council with a new appreciation of the Lord's concern for us. Because of His loving desire to make us like Him, His laws are clear and precise. The rewards for obedience are clearly enumerated, as are the penalties for transgression. In His mercy and love, the Lord has clearly outlined the necessary procedures to be followed so that a person guilty of serious sin may have the satisfaction of going before His legal representatives and receive an official judgment. How blessed we are to have these guidelines so clearly established. How awful it would be to have our status in the Church left to the opinion or whims of men (See Alma 42:22-26).

TELLING THE CHILDREN

After the two-hour council proceedings, we returned home to tell our children about it and the decision of the court. We did so because this would affect our whole family and they needed to know what was going on. We also hoped they would be able to lend their love and support to their dad as he struggled to become worthy to be reinstated in the Church in some future day. The challenge was to tell them in such a way that it would teach them the seriousness of sin and covenant-breaking, yet build their testimonies of the great love of God for each of His children.

None of them knew where we had been that night or why. We had only told them we were going to "a meeting." (That was a natural reason for our absence because I was then serving as Ward Relief Society president, and consequently, was involved in lots of "meetings.") Until this night, none of the children except our oldest son, Don, had known anything about Gerald's unfaithfulness to me.

First we took our eighteen-year-old son and the two oldest girls, ages seventeen and fifteen, into the privacy of a room away from the rest of the family where Gerald explained what he had done and that he had been excommunicated from the Church. Of course they didn't know what that would mean for our family, so he explained the ramifications that had just been outlined to us by the stake president. We warned them that it would probably take years to make things right and get back into the Church. He pled with them to remain strong and to never let this happen to them. Both girls wept with us as they struggled to comprehend the terrible significance of the unbelievable words they were hearing. Along with our son, they all put their arms around Gerald and promised their love and forgiveness.

Next we took each of the middle children, ages twelve, ten, and seven, one by one and explained the situation, Gerald again asking each of them for their forgiveness. He pledged his intention to repent and to become a real part of the family. Our twelve-year-old daughter, the one who had cried so hard when he dropped out of Church attendance, thought he had been excommunicated for not attending church, and said, "But I thought you had to do adultery or something serious like that." After explaining that was exactly what he had done, she sobbed even harder. She just could not believe that her dad could have done such a thing. [Later, Gerald asked her if she had worried about what her friends might say or do. She said, "No way! All I was worried about was keeping you and Mom together so there would be no divorce."]

All of the children were fantastic. Not one of them condemned Gerald nor withdrew their love from him. They readily forgave him and pledged their support. Throughout the coming years of darkness and turmoil, they prayed for him; they believed in him; they tried to encourage him; and somehow, even as they suffered his slings and arrows, they managed to keep welcoming him into the family.

As people became aware of what had happened, we were very concerned for our children, being fearful that some of their friends and classmates might avoid them or withdraw their friendship because of his excommunication. We did their friends an injustice, however, because they were great! Never once did anyone hurt or offend our children because of Gerald's situation. In fact, just the opposite was true.

OUR CHILDREN'S PERSPECTIVE

Over twenty years ago, as I was writing *The Worth of A Soul*, I asked each of the older children to tell me what advice I should include for the children and families of others who were just learning about excommunication. They each took the question seriously and gave it much thought before responding. The consensus of their response was as follows:

1. Never give up hope.
2. Show your love all the time.
3. Let them (the excommunicant) know you are on their side.
4. Try not to judge.
5. Always stick by them and don't give up, or it will be a lot harder for him.
6. Be understanding. So a mistake was made. We all make mistakes. Show the same love and support as before.
7. Always pray for them.

Church disciplinary councils can provide healing and a starting point for our return to Heavenly Father. But if one is rebellious, or doesn't understand the purpose of such a council, it can be a very fearful and confusing experience, both to the person who has sinned, as well as to the family members. Because it is so easy to misunderstand the love which Heavenly Father has built into this process of correction, in Appendix B we share some principles involved in the Church court system that might be helpful.

> Therefore, he giveth this promise unto you, with an immutable covenant that they shall be fulfilled; and all things wherewith you have been afflicted shall work together for your good, and to my name's glory, saith the Lord [D&C 98:3].

CHAPTER NINE

BUFFETED

It would be a serious error to think one could somehow make an excommunication a comfortable experience. Suffering is an essential part of the repentance and learning process. As difficult as life had been for our family in the past, those painful experiences were as nothing compared to the hell that dominated our lives the first few years after the excommunication. It is not possible to fully describe what it was like for us then, but I will try to provide some glimpses to illustrate the principles we learned from that experience.

This mortal life is a school. It is designed to teach us the lessons we need to prepare ourselves to return to our Heavenly Father. We came to this mortal life with the expectation and agreement, indeed, even the *anticipation* of experiencing the critical "opposition in all things," without which we could not learn, grow and become like our Father in Heaven. (See 2 Nephi 2:11-15.) To become like Him is a huge assignment and requires an enormous amount of spiritual "home-work," including pain and suffering, much of which may seem unfair and undeserved.

We understood that, in addition to the natural opposition that comes from living in an imperfect world, part of our homework would require us to face and overcome relentless opposition from Lucifer and those who follow him with cruel determination to make us like *them*, instead of like Father. "*And it was given unto him to make war* with the saints, and to overcome them; and power was given him over all kindreds, and tongues, and nations" (Revelation 13:7).

This "war" involves a much greater threat to us than mere tempta-tions.[1] Peter likened Lucifer's vicious hatred to the prowling of a

---

1 How an improper perception of the necessity of temptations can defeat us is shown
   in the chapters "The Battleground of Temptation," in *Putting On The Armor of God*,
   and "The Goliath of Temptation," in *Conquering Your Own Goliaths*.

ferocious, wild lion: "Be sober," he warned, and "be vigilant, because your adversary the devil, as a roaring lion, walketh about, seeking whom he may devour" (1 Peter 5:8). If he could, Satan would destroy every person on earth, both spiritually and physically. "There is no crime he would not commit, no debauchery he would not set up, no plague he would not send, no heart he would not break, no life he would not take, no soul he would not destroy" (*Messages of the First Presidency*, comp. James R. Clark, 6 vols., S. L. C., Utah: Bookcraft, 1965-75, 6:179).

Fortunately the Lord has placed limitations on what the devil and his demons are allowed to do in their attacks against us. For example, he is inhibited in his ability to tempt children before the age of accountability (See D&C 29:47). He can never tempt us beyond our present capacity to resist (See 1 Corinthians 10:13). He is able to put thoughts and suggestions into our minds,[2] but he is not allowed to read our thoughts (see D&C 6:16), and he can never force a person to do something to which they have not agreed.

But all of that changes when a person is excommunicated. In that case, the person is not only expelled from membership in Christ's Church, but he is also delivered over to "the buffetings of Satan."

> Inasmuch as ye are cut off for transgression, ye cannot escape the buffetings of Satan until the day of redemption.
>
> And I now give unto you power from this very hour, that if any man among you . . . is found a transgressor and repenteth not of the evil, that ye shall deliver him over unto the buffetings of Satan . . . [D&C 104:9 -10. See also 78:12; 82:21; 132:26].

What does this awesome warning mean? Webster's Dictionary of Synonyms identifies the word "buffet" with other vindictive words such as beat, pound, pummel, thrash and thresh. The "buffetings of Satan" are an expansion and intensification of what he is otherwise allowed to inflict on people who are not under Church discipline. As Bruce R. McConkie explained:

> To be turned over to the buffetings of Satan is to be given into his hands; it is to be turned over to him with all the protective power of the priesthood, of righteousness, and of godliness removed, *so that Lucifer is free to torment, persecute, and afflict such a person without let or hindrance.* When the bars are down, the cuffs and curses of Satan, both in this world and in the world to come,

---

2 See discussion of this in Chapter Seven.

bring indescribable anguish typified by burning fire and brimstone. The damned in hell so suffer [*Mormon Doctrine*, 2nd Ed., Salt
Lake City, Utah: Bookcraft, Inc., 1966, p. 108; emphasis added].

I suppose that these are merely words to a person who has never
suffered through this type of experience, but those words send shivers
of fear down my spine just remembering what it was like for me. Alma,
who had rebelled against the Church and his prophet father, experienced these buffetings for three days. His description was: "I was in the
darkest abyss . . . I was racked with eternal torment, for my soul was
harrowed up to the greatest degree and racked with all my sins. Yea, I
did remember all my sins and iniquities, for which I was tormented
with the pains of hell . . . The very thought of coming into the presence of my God did rack my soul with inexpressible horror" (See
Mosiah 27:29; Alma 36: 12, 13, 15).

Two of our former church presidents have tried to describe the
difficulty of this intensified tutoring. President Joseph Fielding Smith
said: " . . . to be turned over to the buffetings of Satan unto the day of
redemption . . . must be something horrible in its nature. Who wishes
to endure such torment? No one but a fool! *I have seen their anguish. I
have heard their pleadings for relief and their pitiful cries that they cannot
endure the torment*" (*Doctrines of Salvation*, Compiled by Bruce R.
McConkie, 6th Ed., Salt Lake City, Utah: Bookcraft, Inc., Vol. II, p. 97).
And President Harold B. Lee said, "One of the greatest and saddest
things that we can see is one who has had the Spirit of the Lord and
then has lost it by sin, and they stand now in the dark and are turned
over to the buffetings of Satan, and then experience the torture cham-
bers of the hell in which they must live, which is terrible indeed as the
Lord has warned" (*Ensign*, Jan. 1974, p. 101).[3]

Other prophets have described the torment caused by Satan's

---

3 Why would a kind and loving God do this? Because of His stubborn and infinite
love for us, the Lord will use whatever drastic means he can devise to wake us up
to the need for change—even such drastic and life-threatening measures as famines,
plagues or excommunication. They are all divine "wake-up calls," designed as last-
ditch attempts to help us learn and repent when all else has failed. For example, "If
she [referring to wayward members of the church] observe not to do whatsoever I
have commanded her, I will visit her according to all her works, with sore affliction,
with pestilence, with plague, with sword, with vengeance, with devouring fire"
(D&C 97:26). Nephi understood the principle behind these "last ditch" efforts to
help people use their agency more effectively. And thus "Nephi did cry unto the
Lord, saying: O Lord, do not suffer that this people shall be destroyed by the sword;
but O Lord, rather let there be a famine in the land, to stir them up in remembrance
of the Lord their God, and perhaps they will repent and turn unto thee" (Helaman
11:3-4). It is the same with the "buffetings" of Satan.

"buffetings" by likening it to the agony of being placed in a lake of fire and brimstone, having fiery darts thrown at our bodies, or comparing it to the overpowering force of whirlwinds, hail, and mighty storms beating upon us. Still others have referred to the devastating effect of Satan's buffetings as being held captive in a "gulf of misery and endless wo."[4] Each of these attempts to describe Satan's buffetings provides the reader with a tiny glimpse of what it is like to be in Satan's power. I will now attempt to add my own view.

During the black years that followed my excommunication, I was much like a marionette under Satan's control. It seemed that whenever his hosts of evil spirits felt the need of some entertainment, they could pull my strings and know that I would perform according to their will. That may sound overly dramatic, but the demons we invite into our lives by repeatedly making wrong choices are highly skilled in helping us perpetuate those choices until we reach the point of enslavement and lose our agency. "It is as though Satan ties strings to the mind and body so that he can manipulate one like a puppet," said Richard G. Scott (*Ensign*, May 1986, pp. 10-11).

In addition to enormous discouragement and erosion of hope, the demons constantly put pornography into my path and encouraged me to use it. If there was a discarded magazine along the road, I often stopped to see if it was pornographic. Over time it seemed that I developed a skill of knowing when to stop and look and when not to stop. In fact, I became so accurate that I marveled at the "psychic" ability I had developed. Of course, I now know that it was the whisperings of the evil spirits who constantly accompanied me, intent upon my destruction, that I learned to "hear."

I am still amazed by their power to manipulate and influence the circumstances of our lives. Several days after I returned home, confessed, and started trying to build a new relationship with my wife, an event occurred which left me trembling in absolute terror. It was Satan's first direct manifestation of his power to destroy me since my sins had made me subject to his "buffetings." This was "round one" in my forthcoming battles with Satan and it occurred one morning as I was leaving for work.

During those initial days, as we awaited word about the pending disciplinary council, LoAnne and I had been extremely cautious in the

---

4 See 2 Nephi 9:19, 26; Jacob 6:10; Ephesians 6:16; 1 Nephi 15:24; D&C 247:17; Alma 26:6; Helaman 5:12; 2 Nephi 1:13; Helaman 3:29; 5:12.

way we treated each other. There had been no serious disagreements or conflicts, but things were, understandably, quite tense between us. Then, on this particular morning, we suddenly found ourselves engaged in an unexpected argument over something trivial and unimportant. Pent up emotion and fear caused the disagreement to grow until we were very angry with one another and we exchanged unkind and hurtful words. To make matters worse, I felt pressured by time because I was late for an appointment. I had to leave—we would just have to settle things later.

As I left the house, I was alarmed at the unexpected intensity of our feelings. It was obvious that our wounds went deeper than I had supposed. As I got into my car, the confidence I had been feeling that things were going to be all right between us plummeted into a nerve-shattering fear and uncertainty that made me wonder if we could ever affect a genuine reconciliation. The barriers we faced in rebuilding our marriage were greater than I had realized—perhaps even insurmountable.

I trembled at the thought of struggling through the day on this shaky foundation as I drove the half-block from our house to the cross street, but there, incredibly, I came upon the woman with whom I had sinned. She was driving right to our house!

The first few days after I ended our brief relationship, she had called me at the house over a dozen times. Though it was difficult, I had done as I promised and refused to listen to her or to talk to her. Each time she called I told her I was sorry, but I could no longer talk to her. I had promised a total break, and I meant to honor my promise. The calls had finally stopped and we thought she had given up, but here she was, just seconds from our house. We saw each other simultaneously and stopped our cars right in the street. In astonishment, I got out and walked to her car to ask what in the world she was doing here. She tried to pull me through her window to kiss me. As I pulled away from her, she began to plead for a chance to win me back. She kept pleading and telling me how happy we would be together. She insisted that she wanted me badly enough to actually come to my house!

I knew this had to end here and now, once and for all. I attempted to reason with her, but she began to cry, and I found my heart melting for her. Fresh as I was from the disconcerting argument with my wife, her flattering pleas were very enticing. I could hear voices echoing in my mind, urging me, "*Go with her. Go with her. You deserve it. Go with her and be happy."* I came within a hair's breadth of yielding to her, but I knew full well that any further compromise would reverse my effort to repent and doom any chance I had to salvage my marriage. Her pleading was almost more than I could bear, but somehow, I found the strength to ignore her tears and tell her angrily that this could never be. She must never contact me again. I walked back to my car and drove away, hoping she would do the same. Now I was crying, too.

I was so confused and disoriented that I could hardly drive. I had just left the house, shaken because of my reaction to the unexpected argument with my wife, afraid of what lay ahead in our future together. My fear was increased as I discovered my susceptibility to this woman's pleadings. It was frightening to see how weak my commitments were.

About two hours later, lights began to flash and bells rang in my mind as I suddenly recognized the incredible timing with which that seemingly coincidental meeting had taken place. Had I left my house one minute later, the woman would have been at our front door, in confrontation with two people already angry with each other. What a disaster to our shaky marriage that would have been! Had I left ten seconds sooner, I would never have seen her coming and my wife would have been left to confront her, and the temptation would never have touched me. I broke into a sweat as I realized that not only was the timing incredible, but for the meeting to occur immediately following our first big argument was beyond the possibility of coincidence.

I knew with positive certainty that this had all been engineered by Satan. With a sickening feeling of dread, I felt the terror of being subject to the awesome power and determination of the adversary. I shrank as I realized that his buffetings were not to be merely a series of temptations or trials. This was to be all-out war! Imagine the horror of having to face such an enemy for months, and perhaps years, without the priesthood, without the Holy Ghost. It seemed to me that Satan had all the weapons, and that I was unarmed. I was absolutely panic-stricken.

During those first years I was, from time to time, inflicted with the most horrible and inexplicable emotions. When these ferocious attacks came upon me, my emotions would change in just a few seconds from normal rationality to a nearly insane rage of bitterness and poison so overwhelming that it almost choked me. Being so suddenly filled with incomprehensible darkness and evil emotions, and not understanding the source of those feelings, I would find myself lashing out with this vicious venom upon whoever was near, which was usually my family, and most often my wife. What a terrifying experience it was to find myself suddenly transformed from a normal "day-to-day" person to one possessed of poison, hate, bitterness, and mental anguish so violent that it felt like my brain was churning inside my skull.

When this evil influence took possession of me, it was as if I could stand beside myself in the same room and observe what was happening—as if I were another person. It was as if I were required to stand there and watch this awful behavior as a part of my punishment. And as I watched in horror, I seemed to hear a divine whisper: "*See what your pride and selfishness and disobedience have brought upon you and your family? Now, can you see that it is wiser to yield yourself unto My will than to become a servant and slave to Satan, your enemy?*"

I never understood that almost vicarious experience until I noticed Lehi's similar description of his experience in the "mists of darkness." He didn't say that he was in darkness, or that he experienced darkness, but that "*I beheld myself* that I was in a dark and dreary waste" (1 Nephi 8:7). That's what it was like for me. I would stand there marveling at how *he* (myself) could suddenly act so horribly for no apparent reason. I would shudder in amazement and shame at the way that *he* (myself) was treating the family. Helplessly, what little was left of my decency would protest that this creature could not be me! *It must be a nightmare! This cannot be happening!* My anguished soul would be crying that I didn't want to be that way. I didn't want to act that way. I didn't want this to happen. Yet, under the punishing effect of the demon's buffetings, I was helpless to resist, for I knew not how. Sometimes these attacks would be over in a few hours, but often the raging torment would last for days before wearing off.

Back then, it never occurred to me that what we were suffering was part of my punishment, that it was part of the penalty, part of the painful learning experience which I had demanded by my disobedience. I did not realize how serious it is to "mock God" by breaking our covenants, or that it was a form of pride to believe that one can find happiness outside the boundaries of God's plan for us. Blinded by my justifications and rationalizations, I had not noticed the warnings: "Their transgressions will I bring down with sorrow upon their own heads" (Enos 1:10). The Lord will not tolerate prolonged and deliberate transgression. "I will not succor my people in the day of their [intentional and repeated] transgression," He warned, "but I will hedge up their ways that they prosper not; and their doings shall be as a stumbling block before them" (Mosiah 7:29).

Alma said that sometimes, if a person is compelled to be humble, they will choose to repent. (See Alma 32:13) This is part of the purpose and process of Church discipline. Before an excommunicant can be healed, the pride and foolish ignorance that put him into that situation must be broken and crushed by things which he suffers, so that he can learn, even as a little child, that Heavenly Father really does know best after all. (See D&C 19:15-17) I can now understand why President Harold B. Lee said, "It seems to me, that there comes a time in the lives of those who have sinned so seriously that, short of disciplinary action, I think some men can't repent until they are turned over to the buffetings of Satan by the loss of the Spirit of the Lord" (Priesthood Board Meeting, March 1, 1972, p. 12, as quoted in *Ensign*, May 1974, p. 30). Looking back, I am thankful the Lord loved me enough to provide that remedial course-work, or intensified tutoring.

The "buffetings" I suffered were deserved; they were my own fault. They were painful, but necessary lessons of what it is like to be fully subject to Satan's torment, so that, hopefully, I would not allow that condition to continue into eternity. But my wife and children certainly did not deserve the contentious spirit and frustrations which I inflicted upon them. My children endured untold suffering because of my behavior. Two events may provide glimpses into some of what they endured. Shortly after a heated exchange of criticism between LoAnne and me, which erupted in front of some of our children, I found one of my teenage daughters sitting at my desk in the den writing a letter. She looked so pained and desperate that, in spite of my personal frustrations, I couldn't help but put my hand on her shoulder and ask what was wrong. She immediately broke into heartrending sobs. Nothing I could say can better portray the hardship placed upon the children during the "buffeting period" of the excommunication than these words from her letter.

Dear Grandma,

Things have been going so rotten. If only you were here, everything would seem to be okay. Mom and Dad—when they get into fights, it really makes me cry. I am writing this while they are mad at each other.

Right now I feel like bursting out yelling all of my problems instead of holding them deep within myself. I just can't seem to go talk to my parents anymore. If only you were here so I could talk with you.

Oh, Grandma, I pray and pray and pray for them, but nothing seems to work. What should I do?

My guilty heart was cut to the quick. For a brief moment I was able to see through my own pain, to glimpse the family's torment clearer than my own, and I promised her that I would try to do better. I really meant it, but none of my promises lasted very long in those dark days. I am sure that the prayers of this brokenhearted girl and the other children had a lot to do with the divine endowment of patience which was subsequently given to my wife.[5]

There was another event that was caused by the evil spirit that emanated from me. Our home had a large, upstairs bedroom which was used by three of our daughters. Because tax season was over and I had a new job where I worked the night shift, I would sleep up in their room during the day, where I could be away from the family noise. One day I had a terrible dream about my nine-year-old daughter, whose bed I used. I dreamed that I had slipped over the edge of a very deep chasm. As I hung there, clinging to the cliff, this nine-year-old daughter came running to help me. But she also slipped and fell past me into the chasm toward certain death. In dumbfounded terror I screamed her name as I helplessly watched her fall. As her body fell further and further from my sight, I could hear her calling to me, "I love you, Dad . . . I love you, Dad."

I awoke from the dream in a cold sweat. I could not go back to sleep. That the dream was significant, I was certain, but what could it mean? Were we going to lose her to a premature death? Was she going to fall away from the Church as I had? The meaning of the dream was made plain to me when I told LoAnne about it. She pointed out that my daughter's symbolic fall was related to my spiritual fall. If I had not been in jeopardy, she would not have perished. LoAnne then confided to me that for some time this young daughter had complained of feeling the presence of evil spirits who were "putting bad thoughts in her mind," especially when she was trying to go to sleep. Among other things, they told her not to pray, not to read the scriptures, and not to

---

5 That endowment of grace will be described in the next chapter.

believe her teachers at Church. She was also awakened by terrifying dreams. The torment was so persistent, and she was so often frightened by these Satanic whisperings that she frequently left her bed and joined LoAnne in our bedroom to feel safe again.

The link between her undeserved torment and mine was obvious when I realized that the evil influence of my rampant lust and pornographic fantasies lingered not only in their room where I slept, but most particularly with that bed in which we slept at different times. No doubt there were many evil spirits who frequented this bedroom to take vicarious pleasure in my sin and distress. When I was gone, they busied themselves tormenting her.

Truly, no person can claim that the effect of their sin is limited to their own life! We cannot hide the effect of what we are from our loved ones, nor can we hide the influence of our secret desires. The Spirit of the Lord cannot dwell within the walls of a home where pornography is being viewed, and it is an open invitation to devilish spirits to come and dwell therein.

That dream caused me to feel a sorrow for my daughter that I could not feel for myself. I never used her bed again, and after she received a priesthood blessing from her grandfather, the evil spirits no longer troubled her. How I envied her blessing.[6] I knew that it would protect her, but I also knew that in my wickedness I was beyond protection. I still had much to learn before I would understand how to prepare myself to accept the love and newness of life that the Savior would share with me.

About a year and a half after my excommunication, my wife and children attended her family's reunion. Because of my job, I was not able to attend, nor would I have wanted to if I could. I didn't want to be around anyone, especially happy people, and her family was always happy! At that reunion her family decided to fast weekly and pray for me. Even though this loving effort on my behalf was unknown to me, it really made a difference! My heart began to soften. My resolves and determination were strengthened. Bitterness began to recede, and new hope came into my life. My thinking became clearer, and I began to discover things about myself that I had never understood. I began to see past my sexual preoccupations to other things that could improve life, both for me and for my family.

---

6 LoAnne's father was one of the finest men I have ever known. One of his many efforts to help was an incredible letter he wrote me. See Appendix I.

Later, when LoAnne revealed to me that her family had been fasting and praying for me for several months, I was surprised and moved by their compassion and concern. I was amazed at the effect it had upon me. The total effect of their fasting on my behalf was so profound that I sent a letter to each of them in appreciation. Two paragraphs from that letter follow:

> I feel a tremendous change in my attitude and perception of my problems. It seems I have been stumbling in the dark and didn't know it. I am discovering that the sexual addictions that I thought were my main problems—and on which I focused all of my attention for all these years—are actually more the *symptoms* than the *cause*. In the last few weeks I have become aware of many other areas in my character and personality that are crying for change and improvement . . .

> I know it will take considerable time for me to learn the necessary lessons and develop the proper habits of attitude and performance, but I no longer feel hopeless and defeated. I now have a new confidence and sense of direction. I hope and pray that I have permanently escaped the curse of wavering vacillation and can keep my feet firmly on the path toward the Lord.

One can see from this letter that my thoughts and emotions were turning in the right direction—away from my own limitations and toward the grace and power of the Lord. I would eventually discover that He is the only way that any fallen, mortal man can conquer his 'natural man' nature. I had, at last, caught a glimpse of the real solution to my problems.[7] But to my surprise, the buffetings were far from over.

There seems to be a principle of opposition that the harder we try to do what is right, the harder the demons work to oppose us. Satan took this letter as a warning sign that I was slipping from his grasp. Surrounding me with evil spirits, he launched an overwhelming attack that drove me right back into the jaws of the filthy hell that had become so familiar to me. Like a toothpick before a bulldozer, I crumbled before his invasion. In less than four months I fell from the spiritual height and hope expressed in that letter to the rock-bottom depths of darkness and despair. By "rock-bottom" I mean that I was ready to try drugs, alcohol, suicide, or anything else that I could use to escape the pain of having to live with myself and with my failure. I thought I had been so close to full recovery, but as I stumbled through this

---

7 How this was to come about will be described in Chapter Twelve.

intensified darkness and confusion, I knew I was drowning. As my hopes were dashed and my filthiness returned, I felt totally defeated and hopeless.

That awful vulnerability to Satan's buffetings hung over me like a constant dark cloud for more than two years. Feeling like a rubber band stretched to the breaking point, my emotions were constantly tensed, just waiting and wondering when the next attack would come. I might go for several weeks without a spell, and then suddenly, like a whirl-wind and without warning, Satan would invade and occupy again.

I have since realized that, while we have jobs and families to care for, houses and yards to maintain, the need for sleep and rest and other endless tasks that consume our time, the demons have nothing else to do but tempt and torment us twenty-four hours a day. No wonder we are so frequently admonished to read the scriptures and to "pray always."

Mere words cannot describe those experiences adequately. I know that I have failed to accurately communicate the awful horror which we experienced, and my heart aches for the many families who may be groping their way through similar buffetings in blindness as we did. I must conclude that a true understanding of such experiences is reserved for those who, by their improper choices, place themselves in the sad condition of firsthand exposure. To the rest it will remain an experience which they will never completely fathom. I only hope that what I have tried to describe will help the reader to have compassion and understanding for those who are suffering through it.

That my family could stand by me and continue to believe in me when I was in such an awful state of mind and spirit is a miracle for which I thank my Heavenly Father. The unbelievable constancy of my family's patient support and their belief in me, even in the face of my verbal abuses, beamed brightly as evidence of God's love for me. I can-not count the number of times when their love and patience was all that I had to cling to until I learned to cling to Him.

What I learned through the buffetings applies to every person involved in this mortal war. Satan hates us and is determined to defeat us, and he will do everything in his power to destroy our chances of obtaining the celestial kingdom. On the other hand, Jesus Christ loves us and will do whatever it takes to rescue us from our defeats, to teach us how to fight our battles with Satan (and will lend us the strength to do so), and to return us to our heavenly home.

The Savior's goal is to cleanse and perfect us, so that we can share in the perfect joys of eternity, while the devil's goal is to keep us in sin and defeat, so that he can rule over us in spiritual captivity and misery for eternity. You and I stand between these two opposing powers and every day, with every choice, we cast the deciding vote.

CHAPTER TEN

AN ENDOWMENT OF GRACE

Though my life seemed very difficult throughout those buffeting years, I had many blessings. My children were largely healthy, intelligent and spiritually inclined. They excelled in many areas and I took great pleasure in mothering them and sharing in their achievements. Life, for me, was filled with homework help, parent/teacher conferences, recitals, music practices, ball games, church socials and other events, and very rewarding and fulfilling callings in the Relief Society and Primary organizations. The children were also mostly happy. They were, however, very negatively and sadly affected by the incidents of quarreling and unhappiness they observed between Gerald and me. Thankfully, there were also observable times of good will and good nature between the two of us, but as time went on and the power of his addictions increased, those good times between us became more and more rare.

My journal throughout that time period is filled with entries of specific answers to prayer, of inspiration and help from above. The major root problems in our marriage and our lives would not be resolved for several more years, but the Lord never left me alone through the trials. Whenever I turned to Him in humility and faith, He was there. I knew that He knew me and cared for me and that knowledge sustained me through the difficult times and gave me the courage to keep trying, even when everything seemed to fall apart. I had then, as I have now, a very strong testimony of God's love and care for each of us. I did not then suspect how much I would need to rely on this testimony in the trials that awaited me.

Following are selected passages from my journal during that time period, which reflect some of the things I learned as I suffered through the buffeting years.[1] For example, it was immediately obvious to me that the children would be affected by the excommunication in ways that would require them to

---

1 Because these entries are selected for relevance to our subject, much of the day-to-day activities and normal stresses of the daily mothering of eight children and their respective needs and activities must be supplied by the reader's imagination.

understand and act beyond their years. When the excommunication first became
public knowledge . . .

13 April   Each one of the older children felt the need to talk with
me alone. Gerald had just chastised Tracy rather severe-
ly for something trivial. I reminded her that when he'd told
her of his sin and his desire to repent, that he'd asked for
her help and support. This undeserved chastisement was
exactly the sort of thing she had agreed to understand
and forgive. We are now beginning to see the difference
that having, or not having, the gift of the Holy Ghost
makes in a person. They are less understanding and
more prone to lose their temper and we need to be willing to overlook the hurt it causes us. It seemed to help her
and she was thankful for the explanation.

Don, our oldest, had been suffering under the effects of
Satan, the past week as manifested by his unnatural
impatience and intolerance of the younger children. He
desired a priesthood blessing to help him set a proper
example and to righteously lead the way as the only
priesthood bearer in the family. So we went together to
the bishop's home (also our newly assigned home
teacher) where he received a beautiful blessing.

Then I learned how easy it is to doubt yourself, and consequently, how nec-
essary it is to constantly run evaluation checkups on your own attitudes and
standing before the Lord. When we told Gerald's family about his excommuni-
cation . . .

18 April   . . . he wanted me to talk to his sister while he took time
to have a private talk with his brother. I tried to explain it
to her, but it didn't turn out well. She seemed to want me
to accept the blame for it—she said I was such a domi-
nating person and such a poor wife that I drove him to do
what he did. She also seemed to think that everyone; me,
the children, the bishop and the ward, was setting themselves up as self-righteous judges of him. I hotly denied
that charge—it was absolutely false. But her first charge
about my culpability in the affair really unnerved me—I
had no reply. It deeply hurt me that she felt that way, but
it also frightened me—could it be true?

I soon came to understand that the root problem in all our troubles—our
marriage, Gerald's addictions and extra-marital affair—was selfishness. I have

come to understand that this immature and devilish trait is at the root of all discord in human relations, and that all of us, to some extent, have this problem.

23 April	I got quite upset with Gerald because I felt he had deceived me on a certain matter that came to light last night. I wondered why something as comparatively "small" as this is so hard to forgive. A forgiving spirit seems just as hard to come by this time as the last. I wish forgiveness came natural to me, but it is a struggle each time something comes up. However, with the Lord's help I'll do it, for today I am resolved to be able to partake of the sacrament worthily, having forgiven all.

Gerald is having a real struggle against Satan and it is very rough for him. We are both frightened about the outcome. I certainly don't want to make it any harder for him. I need to be more selfless. Therein lies the key to true forgiveness—think of the other person's needs and hardships instead of your own and develop compassion. Forgiveness follows naturally.

8 May	Gerald and I had another "discussion" about the sad state of our marriage. As President Kimball described in his book, *Marriage*, we have let ours grow stale and unfulfilling to both of us. But through our talking I determined that the root of our problems is just like President Kimball said, selfishness. Both Gerald and I are basically selfish—maybe all people are—but I truly believe, as the prophet said, that any marriage problem can be solved if both partners live the gospel, continue their courting, and cultivate the virtue of unselfishness.

Gerald was reluctant to believe all our problems could be summed up that simply, and he was very discouraged about the whole thing, but I asked his forgiveness and forbearance with me for a while longer and he agreed. I'm glad I have this opportunity of developing that virtue in my life to a greater extent—and for the absolute necessity of it, else I would not recognize it or I would put it off. This is one of the reasons I'm glad I married Gerald. He'll get me to the celestial kingdom yet!

Throughout the buffeting years, life was a roller coaster:

10 June   Gerald told me about some of the terrible temptations he suffered today. His battles with Satan are very real and he wins only at great cost to his morale and strength. I used to feel very assured of his eventual rebaptism and thought it was just a matter of waiting out the time. But tonight I became very frightened and realized his eventual triumph is not at all assured.

25 June   I think Gerald and I are doing a lot better. He's surely a lot more thoughtful of me and helpful at home and I surely do appreciate him a lot more. I hope he feels as happy about our improvement as I do.

2 July   Satan got to Gerald and I again Friday evening and we selfishly coddled our own feelings at the expense of our unity. He surely knows how to manipulate us, but fortunately, we recognized it after only a few hours. I pray the Lord will continue to help us recognize the devil's encroachments upon our marriage and that we can overcome him and ourselves and make our union celestial. It's a discouraging struggle at times, but if I can keep the end in mind and have faith in its eventual fulfillment, it's easier.

When Gerald and I were at his disciplinary council, the stake president suggested that a large part of Gerald's stress was the financial debt and insecurity we had labored under through the past several years. He suggested that it might be necessary for me to help out in that area in order to take some of the stress off his shoulders. So, with Gerald's encouragement, I decided to go to work for a year in order to get us out of debt and to help support our large family. It seemed right at the time and, while I knew there were disadvantages, I felt that a year wasn't so terribly long. I obtained a position working nights so that I could be home with my children during the day.

30 July   After just a couple of weeks, I feel confused and upset about my decision to work. I have shed many tears over the last few days because:

      1—I'm having trouble staying awake at work because I don't get adequate sleep during the day at home;

      2—I'm troubled with constant pain in my neck, shoulder, arm and back at work;

      3—While Tracy is doing an admirable job caring for the

needs of the children at home, she can never fill a mother's shoes nor supply their spiritual/emotional needs all the time I'm sleeping;

4—There are still the demands of a home, husband and children to meet and I'm doing very poorly in keeping up;

5—Karyn and Wendi are becoming very obstinate, stubborn and intractable with Tracy, and even with me, and are showing signs of personality change, too. It breaks my heart. Now I realize a year is forever in the life of a young child and will have lasting consequences.

I am wondering: Is the sacrifice I am making for my husband worth what I am giving up in my children, my home and my health? But what else can I do??

Another lesson I learned through my experience was that, like Alma and his people,[2] when we are forced to shoulder burdens that we don't want to carry, but which are made necessary by the circumstances of our lives, God will lighten those burdens and strengthen us for the task required at our hands.

19 Feb.   At work, I passed my machine training. I've been an official machine clerk for two weeks now. I enjoy the work a whole lot more than what I was doing. The time there seems to go faster. But it won't be difficult for me to quit when the time comes!

I have had the wonderful good fortune to be called to the position of ward Relief Society Spiritual Living leader.

It had been over a year since I'd gone to work, during which time we'd paid most of our debts, when I made these next entries in my journal. Gerald had felt so relieved by the easing of the financial strain upon him, that he had persuaded me to continue working through to the end of the year.

9 October   I felt the Lord's Spirit with me as I taught the lesson at Relief Society today, and I felt good about it. But as I came home and fed Karyn and Wendi, a terrible feeling of tiredness and depression overcame me. I felt the heavy weight of working, tiredness, and illness settle on me; and the awful guilt of never quite doing all I should do, and of neglecting my children's needs, my husband and my home; and the frustration of being pulled in so

---

2 See Mosiah 24:8-15

many directions with no help from Gerald—and I felt it so strongly that I thought I was going to break down. However, I got a chance to verbalize some of it to Gerald when he woke up and, though he didn't respond in quite the way I'd have liked him to, it nevertheless relieved me somewhat to have put it into words.

Today I taught that the Lord revealed to Emma Smith the order of her priorities to be: 1st personal worthiness, 2nd fulfill her obligations to her husband and family, and 3rd to serve diligently in her church calling (D&C 25). The effectiveness with which we fulfill each of those is interdependent upon the effectiveness which we render the other two. Perhaps that is the root of my troubles. I haven't been doing very well in my #2 assignments. But where do I get the time???

I wonder if what I'm doing is right. I wonder if I've wandered off the path into areas where my priorities and attitudes have become messed up. What can I do to relieve some of the tension and guilt and frustration that is building in me? I see that I've lost the testimony I had that the course of my life is in accordance with the Lord's will. I need to regain that assurance. That better be my first priority! I shall pray about it!

10 October I worked last night, and this morning I got about a forty minute doze before taking Tamara to the dentist at 8:00 a.m. Then I rushed right home in time to go visiting teaching at 9:00. We had three very good visits with our sisters and finished just in time to get home and meet Wendi coming home from kindergarten. I fed the girls some lunch and now I am caring for one of my neighbor's little boys. I think I'll get to bed by 2 or 3 this afternoon. I have to leave for work again at 9 tonight.

No answer yet to my prayer for a conviction that I'm doing what I should be doing. I'll keep praying.

14 October I believe I have been given the answer to my prayers. Ever since I've started praying last week the idea that I should start a nursery school in my home has been growing within me until it has become a conviction. The only question that remains is when? I feel the greatest

urgency to get started, but Gerald feels uncomfortable with anything sooner than the end of the year. I'm praying now for guidance on that issue.

16 October I talked with Gerald and told him I felt I'd received my answer to my prayers. As I'd pondered the "when" part of the question about starting a nursery school, and after praying sincerely for guidance, the realization bore down upon me that the Lord had led me into this whole question of quitting work and doing something else now. If the time now wasn't right, He wouldn't have led me into the strong feelings I've had at this time, but would have waited until the time was right. I feel I must forge ahead with it as soon as possible.

17 October Last night Gerald and I went over the budget together—always a depressing experience—but not so last night. To my delight, he was much more optimistic than usual and he came out of it with very positive feelings about my proposed nursery venture. So now I have a full "go-ahead" from him, as well as his support. Now I can tender my notice to quit work.

Joseph Smith taught that a person must have a knowledge that the course of life which he pursues is according to the will of God in order to have confidence in God,[3] to have faith in God's love and grace. The knowledge that the course of my life was according to His will became very precious to me and, as my journal entry on October 9th shows, it was my first priority. I learned by my own experience that I could make decisions correctly, have strength and conviction enough to do "hard things;" and that I could expect guidance and approbation from God if my course of action continued to be in accordance with His will.

The next few entries demonstrate that the roller coaster ride we were on throughout this period was still in full operation. However, though Gerald's emotions were in a complete up-and-down swing, I had to keep myself on an even keel as I dealt with the day-to-day needs of our home and children, at the same time fielding the extremes of his buffeted personality.

21 October This, being the 3rd Sunday of the month, is a family fast day for Gerald. I think he's doing very well, and though I know there are bad times yet to come I think the worst

---

3 See Lecture Sixth of *Lectures on Faith*

and darkest hours are passed. The first year and 4 months were terrible dark times for both of us. He especially suffered, but now we are full of hope.

1 Nov.   Gerald is having a terrible time again. He gets so discouraged when the temptations come with renewed intensity as they do periodically . . . I surely hope and pray he makes it through this one. It is a terrible struggle for him, made even more fearful by his terrible discouragement.

Today is Primary and this evening is stake meeting for Relief Society. Tomorrow Don comes home *[for his mission preparation and farewell]*. Oh, *when* am I going to get everything done?!

9 Nov.   There is still a great deal to be done, but I feel encouraged because I have been praying regularly and thus getting myself more organized. Gerald is also doing so much better now. He seems to have weathered that last storm with minimal damage. I'm very proud of him as he also seems more willing now to accept the challenges of his fight. Only one more week to work at the post office!!

22 January We went to a Ward Family Home Evening, which was very enjoyable. I was pleased that Gerald elected to come with us and even seemed a bit cheerful. He actually smiled a couple of times—what a joy that was to see!

25 January Gerald still blames me for a great deal of his suffering. His resentments toward me are piled so high that only the Lord will ever be able to remove them. I'm so grateful he feels enough love and responsibility for the children that he is willing to stay with me for their sakes. I'm certain he wouldn't otherwise. It's a heartache to me. But I'm confident that his perceptions are distorted, that he isn't himself and that when he is, he'll like me. I operate on that assumption (hope).

There were many times that it seemed I was simultaneously pulled in opposite directions. Because I had to discount and forgive much of what he said, it seemed to Gerald that I was unfeeling and unloving. Yet, I had to be unfeeling or be terribly hurt. It took a great amount of concentration just to keep from reacting negatively to him and to his exaggerated resentment. I learned that giving love and compassion also opens the door to a vulnerable heart. To protect myself, much of the time I distanced myself emotionally from him. I always tried to be compassionate, but when I was, I paid a price in vulnerability.

26 January We went to the zoo and the kids had a great time. But when Gerald got up today he was more than usually unkind to me. I tried to stay in the background to leave him free to enjoy the children and the outing without reacting in hurt or anger, but it was a terrible strain on me. And Gerald's behavior towards me on the way home and after we got home made me wonder for the first time: "Does he actually hate me??" If that is true—well, the possibility of it is causing me to lose my objectivity. Tonight I am hurting.

Then, finally, came the turning point! This is how it happened for me:

27 January I determined last night to kneel in prayer and, with all the fervor of my soul, to obtain two gifts from God. I waited until all the children were in bed when I could be alone. I had to struggle to feel His Spirit as I prayed. I wanted to be awash with it, but it was denied me. I petitioned the Lord to give me a closer relationship with Him and to help me to feel more keenly my relationship to Him as my Father and my Savior. I must know Him better and love Him more because I desire to be more like Him.

I also asked for a gift of the Spirit, specifically the gift of charity. I feel very strongly that only the possession of that gift will enable me to help Gerald. He needs to be loved in a way and to a degree that I cannot, of myself, do. But if the Lord will grant me that endowment, the pure love of Christ, I think I can help him. I prayed for these two blessings the best that I could and then I prayed for Gerald. I pled with the Lord to forgive him and release him from his suffering. I begged God to root out of him the sin and tendency to sin that causes him so much grief and pain. And I asked for mercy that his buffetings might come to an end.

When my prayer was ended I found I'd been on my knees for over an hour and a half! I felt drained and I felt frustrated. I received no immediate answer, nor even any confirmation that my prayer had been heard.

However, when Gerald came home this morning I knew

my prayer had been heard for he came in to me in a cheerful and loving mood. I knew the Lord had helped him in some way and so I'm certain that when I am ready and it is His will He will bless me with the other things I am seeking.

It was soon after this prayer that Gerald's heart was softened and he listened to a tape our son Don had given him for Christmas. It was then that he learned the astounding truth that the change of nature he was seeking did not depend upon his worthiness or abilities, but rather on his deep need and his submission to Christ.[4]

I knew that my Heavenly Father loved me. I knew He had answered my prayers and guided and strengthened me. But I didn't understand or appreciate the full extent of those blessings throughout the buffeting ordeal visited upon Gerald and upon our household. I didn't realize that there had been angels from beyond the veil by my side to comfort me, to turn me to my Savior, to whisper peace and tolerance to my soul when the arrows of hatred and hurt were slung my way. Nor did I know that they were ministering in like manner to our children. It wasn't until that "extra-terrestrial" help was removed that I came to understand the magnificence and scope of the Lord's endowment of love and grace to our family.[5] The following entry from my journal explains how that happened:

13 August   After Gerald started counseling and began making improvements in his life, I entered a period of depression unlike any I'd ever experienced before. I sank lower in my feelings and became almost unable to function. It was really awful! For about two weeks, all I could do was lie on the couch and brood and wonder what I should be doing. I couldn't even organize my thoughts or formulate any plans for keeping house, caring for the children, etc., etc.

Finally I got on my knees and asked the Lord, "WHY?? What is happening to me??" As I pled for understanding it was given to me. I was told that all through the trials and adversity of Gerald's excommunication and subsequent buffeting by Satan, I had been given extra help from beyond the veil, and strength and power to endure, etc. that were more than mine. But now it was up to me to

---

4   Gerald will explain this in full in Chapter 12.

5   See Appendix C for Gerald's comment on this endowment.

learn to adjust and to grow with Gerald—to improve myself along with him. So the "extra" help had been withdrawn and I needed to readjust and gain control and strength through my own efforts—with the Lord's help, of course.

It overwhelmed me when that aid was withdrawn, but after the Lord was merciful and kind enough to give me the explanation, I began slowly to work my way out of it.

This withdrawal of the endowment affected the whole family. The children's problems also seemed to multiply, and they lost the unnatural tolerance and charity for each other that had been their habit up to this time. All of a sudden, the family harmony we had enjoyed was challenged. Trivial things that had been there all along became stumbling blocks. We were all much more easily offended and little things grew into mountains of discord. Gerald was amazed that, suddenly, I was like a tinderbox and would explode at, what seemed to him, the slightest provocation.

If I had ever felt any self-satisfaction because of my "valiant stoicism" throughout our trials, it was effectively removed by this revelation of myself. On my own, without the help of the Lord, I was nothing—could do nothing "valiant." Moreover, it became obvious that there were many areas in which I needed help to change and improve, just as did Gerald.

The prophet, Ether, taught that, if men (and women) would come to Him, the Lord would show unto them their weaknesses in order that they could be made strong.[6] That is precisely what He was doing for me—showing me my natural weaknesses that I might work to overcome them. Just as in the familiar poem, "Footprints,"[7] I had been carried through the worst time of my life, but when it was ending, God gently put me down to learn to stand on my own. It seemed a brutal lesson at the time, but became the basis on which I could grow and further my progress toward eternal life.

---

6 See Ether 12:27

7 Copyright Margaret Powers 1964

CHAPTER ELEVEN

SURRENDER

Perfect joy and fulfillment are what God desires for each of us. To receive that joy, we must be changed and made into new creatures on the inside rather than merely altering our outward behaviors. This divine and inward transformation sets us free from our demons and gives us the power to control our 'natural man' natures. To begin that change, however, we must first *recognize*—and then *admit*—that without God's help, we will never overcome our faults sufficiently to become able to experience that perfect joy and fulfillment.[1]

There is far more to yielding ourselves to God's higher power than in just giving up our sins. There is a life transforming and liberating difference between being willing to let go of a particular sin (an outward change of behavior), and surrendering all our burdens to the Savior through His Atonement.

If we would be changed by Christ, we must not only yield to Him our will in repentance and obedience, but we must also surrender to Him our other burdens, like self-pity and feelings of worthlessness or inferiority, along with all the hurts, fears, doubts and everything else which is unworthy of one who belongs to Him, and that keeps us from being whole. We must admit and surrender these spiritual infections to Him in total honesty, with nothing held back, for only then can He remove them from our hearts, minds and emotions, making us new and whole. Total healing, then, requires total surrender.

This process of surrender has been scripturally described as coming to Christ with a broken heart and a contrite spirit, acknowledging our unworthiness and nothingness without Him, or as yielding our whole souls to God. Others have described it as "hitting rock-bottom," but that point of helpless despair is often reached without moving to

---

1 The necessity of total honesty in our self-evaluation is discussed in Chapter One, in *Draw Near Unto Me*.

the turning point of surrendering ourselves to Christ's higher power.

Whatever it is called, this process, in which we finally surrender the pride of trying to fix ourselves, is one of consciously choosing to allow the Savior to take care of the fixing and rebuilding. It is surrendering or yielding our prideful self-will to His will; an acknowledgement that He is supreme and we are not. As the Book of Mormon counsels, "Acknowledge your unworthiness before God at all times," and " . . . save they shall cast these things away, and consider themselves fools before God, and come down in the depths of humility, he will not open unto them" (Alma 38:14; 2 Nephi 9:42).

I reached that turning point at Christmastime, almost two years after my excommunication. At last I was able to see myself for what I really was: a filthy slave to my carnal nature, an addict to pornography and masturbation, a failure with my family, my God and myself. I saw myself as I really was: a hopeless, hollow and helpless wretch, a totally miserable creature who hated himself so much that he would prefer not to exist. I also recognized and admitted that I had descended totally into Satan's grasp and that I was tossed about by his desires as helplessly as a twig in a raging torrent.

I knew that my increasingly feeble attempts to repent, restrain my lust and come closer to the Lord were constantly washed away by tidal waves of guilt, shame and hate. I knew I was losing ground—that I was now further away from God and the Church than I was when I had been excommunicated. But even worse than these devastating realizations was the dreadful certainty that it was no longer possible for me to change. I finally recognized that my own power and efforts offered absolutely no possibility of escape from what I had become. I had exhausted my own resources and everything else I had tried. There was no more fight left in me. I was completely wrung dry. And I felt there was no way I could face another year like the last two. I had endured to my limit.

[I want to emphasize that while this was a process of total honesty, it was not a repeat of the self-abasement and condemnation, which for thirty years had chained me to my failures. This was different in that it brought about a release from all my self-imposed and self-defeating burdens.]

As a "last-ditch effort," I went for a long walk near a river, where I could be alone and admit all this to Heavenly Father. I walked and prayed for a long time, admitting all that I had come to realize. I told

Heavenly Father how I had tried to love and obey Him, how hard I had tried to overcome my faults, how I had tried to love my wife and children and how I had tried to forgive myself, expressing sorrow for how miserably I had failed in all these attempts.

More importantly, I admitted to Him that I finally knew that I was, by myself, powerless to save myself, and that unless He reached out to save me, I would most certainly be lost forever. I admitted to Him that after trying and failing for over thirty years, I had little hope or faith that He could save me, but if that unimaginable miracle was somehow possible, it would require pure mercy, for I had absolutely no merit upon which to base my plea.

They were bitter and painful words, but at last I was admitting that I needed a Savior. At last I could plainly see that I could never make myself good enough for God without His help. At last I was surrendering the pride of the false hope that I could, without depending on Him, fix myself. How stubborn I was to resist such a simple lesson! Often the scriptures emphasize that " . . . since man had fallen he could not merit anything of himself," and " . . . there is no flesh that can dwell in the presence of God, save it be through the merits, and mercy, and grace of the Holy Messiah . . ." (Alma 22:14; 2 Nephi 2:8).

There was no confidence in my prayer that day. It was not a petition of faith to a loving Heavenly Father, but more like a drowning man's involuntary cry for help, even though he believes there is no one within miles to hear his plea.

At first, the results of this lengthy prayer were devastating. While I knew I was unworthy of it, I hoped for some kind of loving response like I had experienced on the canal bank two years previously, just before my initial confession. But this time the heavens were silent. I felt no peace or assurance that my prayer was heard.

I fasted that day and the next in an effort to show God I really meant what I said. I wanted Him to know that I knew that I was literally at the end of my rope and had no more strength to hang on. This was the end. My life was now in His hands. Either He would do something, or I would perish, surrendering myself forever to the victorious Lucifer. I continued groping awkwardly, with no real hope of response, certain that the silence only confirmed the hopelessness of my situation.

All this felt so humiliating, like the ultimate failure, when in reality, it was exactly the opposite. What I felt was simply the pain of my stubborn pride and insistence upon fixing myself crumbling away. All those years I had thought I was humble, but guilt and shame are not humility. I was about to discover that I had been guilty of an enormous arrogance that had wasted my life as I tried to substitute my own willpower and the learning of men for the grace and power of Christ. I was about to learn that I needed to repent not only of my sexual sins, but also of the prideful sin of trying to fix my deviant behaviors by myself instead of humbly allowing the Savior to transform my fallen nature.

At last I had gotten myself out of the Lord's way and opened the door to Him. It was the door to His grace and intervention, the door on which (I would later come to understand) He had been knocking through all those dreary years, waiting for me to open to Him so that He could come into my life and rescue me.

Finally, my pitiful life was ready to turn. At last my descent had ended.

CHAPTER TWELVE

A MIGHTY CHANGE

After groping my way through that "last chance prayer" along the river, I came away bitterly disappointed at receiving no response. Though I had no conception of what God could do for me, or how He might answer my prayer, in my rock-bottom desperation I had gone crawling to Him, hoping He could save me from the only alternative I thought I had left—ending my life.

Now I know that God never ignores a sincere prayer. He heard my cry for help just as He hears and answers every sincere prayer. He cared about my desperate plight then just as He cares for the suffering of every one of His children. Whether or not we are presently deserving of His help does not lessen His concern and caring.

I didn't know it at the time, but God had already lovingly provided the answer to my desperate prayer. The solution I needed was on a cassette tape which my son had given me a couple of months before. It was a talk by George Pace, one of his religion teachers at BYU. My heart was hard and I had avoided listening to it. I was sick of reading and listening to things that emphasized ideals I felt I could not live up to. Feeling bored by the long night shift at the Post Office, I finally listened to the tape on headphones one night at work as I sorted mail. I was humbled later to learn that God had softened my heart because of the pleading of my wife.[1] To this day, that first hearing of this tape remains the pivotal experience of my life. Everything in my life is measured by *before* and *after* hearing those words.

AN ASTOUNDING REVELATION

Brother Pace's main idea was that our conception of the gospel is divided into two parts: first, the vast body of "moral and ethical

---

1 See journal entry for 27 January in Chapter Ten.

principles," meaning all the dos and don'ts, most of which are common to every religion, and secondly, the "doctrine of Christ," where we find the power to overcome our faults and become "partakers of the divine nature" (See 2 Peter 1:4). At that time I did not know what was meant by "the doctrine of Christ." I could not recall ever hearing that expression before, even though it is the central theme of *The Book of Mormon*, which mentions that specific phrase over a dozen times!

His tape helped me see the contrast between man's way and God's way of achieving change. The humanistic approach is to work on the moral and ethical principles to overcome our faults and imperfections, working from the outside in. With sufficient willpower and determination, this approach, (which I had been using for so long) can result in the eventual control of our behavior. But only Jesus Christ has the power to change our fallen natures, from the inside out, which enables us to achieve a Christlike level of behavior.

I was surrounded that night by hundreds of fellow employees, but the words on that tape brought my tormented life to a screeching halt. For several moments it was as if time stood still and everything else in my world disappeared. Surrounded by people and machines, my workplace was a very noisy environment, but I heard nothing except a Spirit-born message pounding in every fiber of my awareness: "*This is the answer you have been seeking. Only in Jesus Christ will you find peace and the power to heal your wounds. He has been waiting for you so long. When will you open your life to Him?*" Following are the words on the tape that triggered that message:

> Now in the gospel, in a sense, there are two fundamental breakdowns . . . There is what we refer to as "the doctrine of Christ," and then there is what we refer to as the moral and ethical principles.

> Now, it is in "the doctrine of Christ" that the power comes. And because of the power that can flow in a personal relationship with the Lord; giving our lives to Him, serving Him with all of our hearts; through that power, through the heavenly element of the Holy Ghost, we will acquire a celestial dimension of moral and ethical character.

> But somewhere along the line we come into the Church and we get a testimony, but we get "caught up" in a kind of humanistic approach to solving our personal problems, to changing our behavior. *If we get caught up in the approach of hacking away on the*

moral and ethical principles, we can never, worlds without end, go above and beyond a terrestrial dimension of character in our lives.

But if we accept the Lord and we're filled with His Spirit and *we know that He is the source of the power we need to solve all of our problems,* then the natural accruement to us will be to acquire a kind of honesty, a kind of patience, a kind of love, a kind of integrity that is of a celestial nature . . .

Some of the time I am troubled in my heart when I see men and women who approach the gospel almost as though it is simply a moral and an ethical system. It is all of that, but is much, much more . . . for finally, *it is only He who can change human nature.*

Oh it is true, we can change human behavior, *but changing human behavior is a lot different than changing human nature. And only the blood of Christ can place you and I [sic] in a position to have our nature changed* [George W. Pace, cassette recording, *Developing a Personal Relationship With the Savior,* American Fork, Utah: Covenant Recordings, Inc., 1979].[2]

For the first time in my life, I was aware of the difference between merely controlling human behavior through determination and willpower, and the *actual modification of human nature* through the power of Christ's Atonement, so that we no longer need or desire unworthy behaviors. All my life I had been tormented by the struggle between the spiritual part of me that wanted to love and obey God, and the carnal part of me that craved pornography and masturbation. For the first time, I was glimpsing the astounding idea that through all those years, as I struggled to control my evil behaviors, I had only been "hacking away" at the *symptoms.* But the real problem for me and for everyone else is not our deviant *behaviors,* but our *fallen human natures,* which only the Lord can change.

MY FAITH BEGINS TO GROW

This was the beginning of the transformation process that changed my degraded nature.[3] I certainly did not comprehend what all this meant, but each time I pondered it, the Spirit bore witness to me that it was *here,* in "the doctrine of Christ," that I would find the answers and the power I had been seeking. It was my first glimpse into the

---

2 Unfortunately, no longer in publication.

3 For additional principles on the full *process* of rebirth, see Appendix E.

simple doctrine that I must stop trying to shortcut my way around the Savior with willpower and good works alone; that I, like every person on earth, need the Savior to help me make my way back to the Father.

My escape from Satan's power was not as sudden nor as complete as was Alma's, who, in the very instant of recognizing Christ in his life, was relieved of his anguish and filled with unspeakable joy, peace, and forgiveness (See Alma 36:1-24). But my rescue was just as real and wonderful as his. Slowly, purposefully, step-by-step, the Lord began to work the miracle of His rescue and salvation in my life. Line upon line, never faster than I could receive it, He made me aware of truths I had never recognized before. He began to open the scriptures to my understanding in a manner that built my faith in Christ and made it possible for Him to work within me. He began directing the proper assistance into my life. He raised up friends to help. He awakened me to a life of joy and peace that I had never in my wildest imaginations thought possible.

Even though I had received an unmistakable witness of the Spirit, my weak faith needed further witness and assurance that it was safe to cling to this new "doctrine." In His kindness, the Lord literally flooded me with additional witnesses that increased my faith until it was sufficient to allow me to accept the gift of renewal He offered me. For example, not long after receiving this revelation about Christ being the solution to my problems, I found a Protestant religious tract which bore a second witness to me of the things I had learned from Brother Pace. It said:

> Every religion in the world, except Christianity, boils down to an effort by man to attain heaven by climbing a ladder of goodness and working his way to God. Christianity is unique. The gospel of Jesus stands alone. It alone is a record of God's coming down to man, His condescension in Jesus Christ to provide for man what man could not do for himself.
>
> The scriptures tell us that the wages of sin is death. Because we willingly choose against God—and sin is just that; an attitude of independence from God—the result of our sin is alienation from God, described in the New Testament as spiritual death. A spiritually dead man cannot bring himself back to life [Denomination and author unknown].

As I read those words, I knew they were true. And then, I knew with even greater certainty that I was on the right track, when I found this quote from President N. Eldon Tanner: "The gospel is not merely a moral code of living based on seeking to acquire the attributes of the Savior, *but is also the actual means* [the divine power we need] essential to salvation" (*Ensign*, Apr. 1982, p. 5).

THE ANSWER WAS THERE ALL ALONG

Turning to the scriptures, I found "the doctrine of Christ" to be a major theme—indeed, the very core of the glad tidings of the gospel. With my eyes opened to new insight and understanding, I discovered how blind I had been. Everywhere I looked I found the scriptures describing Christ's power to deliver us from our evil nature. How could I have missed them? There are multitudes of passages that emphasize our absolute dependency upon the Savior if we are ever to escape our evil nature and become worthy to reach the Father. Each new scripture reference added to my knowledge and the faith that I needed to reach out to Him.

I read how "he changed their hearts; yea, *he awakened them out of a deep sleep, and they awoke unto God.* Behold, they were in the midst of darkness; nevertheless, their souls were illuminated by the light of the everlasting word . . ." (Alma 5:7). I found myself experiencing a similar awakening and change. I fastened my hope on the words of King Benjamin's converts, who testified, "We believe all the words which thou hast spoken unto us; and also, we know of their surety and truth, because of the Spirit of the Lord Omnipotent, *which has wrought a mighty change in us, or in our hearts, that we have no more disposition to do evil, but to do good continually*" (Mosiah 5:2). Similarly, King Lamoni's people testified, after being converted through Ammon's teachings, that "their hearts had been changed; that they *had no more desire to do evil*" (Alma 19:33).

Oh, what a "mighty change," indeed! Think of it—no more disposition or desire to do evil! As I repented of my previous indifference to the Savior's sacrifice by trying to save myself, He began His work within me to cast away all that was unholy. As He changed my heart and nature, the Lord took away the awful enslavement to pornography and masturbation that had dominated my life for so long. After all those years it was simply gone! In its place I had a new sense of self-worth and a burning love for my Savior and my Heavenly Father. As I gained an awareness of Their love for me, I became a totally new person.[4]

---

4 For additional principles on every person's need for spiritual transformation, see Appendix D.

I read the Savior's own words about our total and absolute dependence upon Him for access to the Father: "I am the true vine, and my Father is the husbandman. I am the vine, ye are the branches . . . Abide in me, and I in you. As the branch cannot bear fruit of itself, except it abide in the vine; no more can ye, except ye abide in me. If a man abide not in me, he is cast forth as a branch, and is *withered* . . ." (John 15:1, 5, 4, 6. See also 1 Nephi 15:14-15.).

That is so plain and obvious. No wonder my life had been so frustrated and "withered." Although my intentions had been good in my efforts to repent, I could now see how I had spent my life struggling as a separate branch, with no spiritual connection to the Savior, the only true life source. In my efforts to reach the Father, I had ignored the Savior. I had never learned to rely upon Him for the strength and power I needed to overcome my faults. Our job is to build a relationship with the Father through Christ, to increase the flow of nourishment from them, not to go off and start a whole new tree of our own. I had always believed that I must perfect myself before He could accept me. But now I realized that if that were possible, we would not even need a Savior. No man who *deserved* redemption would *need* redeeming. I learned that reliance upon Christ is so necessary that "the Lord God showeth us our weakness that we may know that it is by *his grace*, and *his great condescensions* unto the children of men, that we have power to do these things" (Jacob 4:7).

> And now, my sons, remember, remember that *it is upon the rock of our Redeemer, who is Christ, the Son of God that ye must build your foundation*; that when the devil shall send forth his mighty winds, yea, his shafts in the whirlwind, yea, when all his hail and his mighty storm shall beat upon you, it shall have no power over you to drag you down to the gulf of misery and endless wo, because of the rock upon which ye are built, *which is a sure foundation, a foundation whereon if men build they cannot fall* [Helaman 5:12].

I was learning that my life had been withered and empty because my foundation had been man's wisdom and willpower rather than Christ and His infinite power. It took me a long time to learn this lesson. How stubborn I had been! What unnecessary suffering and pain that stubbornness had caused my family and me! I wondered how I could have been so blind to all this plainness when I had attended church meetings and read scriptures my whole life. I started reviewing the lesson manuals we had used and was astonished to find clear statements like the following, which I had even underlined, though not understood:

> *Only in him can any man find the strength, the power and ability to live a godly life. Only in Christ is there power to transform the human mind and the human heart,* that in a purified state men might attain and enjoy happiness.

> If man is to become like Christ, by means of the Holy Spirit, he must begin to partake of the divine truth and power which Jesus possesses. *A major purpose of Christ's mission* on earth was to reveal his glory to man (John 1:14) and *to give man the divine truth and power required to attain salvation in the presence of God* [*In His Footsteps Today*, Salt Lake City, Utah; Deseret Sunday School Union, 1969, pp. 4, 29].

As I looked for ways to increase my faith in these principles, I learned that Paul taught that our faith in Jesus Christ is proportionate to the degree that we are willing to "hear" the word of God about Christ (See Rom. 10:17). I plunged myself into the scriptures and they became a major factor in my rescue and healing.[5] I stopped just "reading" the words and counting the number of times I read. For the next year and a half, I spent every spare minute searching and studying. My faith that the Savior could, in fact, become my Savior grew by leaps and bounds. I was really getting excited. For the first time in my life I could believe in a true and permanent victory.

It was many years later, when I read the following words by Elder Boyd K. Packer, that I came to understand why changing my focus from a preoccupation with my sin to a focus on the doctrine of Christ had such power to transform my life. He said, "*True doctrine, understood, changes attitudes and behavior.* The study of the doctrines of the gospel will improve behavior quicker than a study of behavior will improve behavior. Preoccupation with unworthy behavior can lead to unworthy behavior. That is why we stress so forcefully the study of the doctrines of the gospel" (*Ensign*, Nov. 1986, p.17). This statement taught me that by focusing on my sinfulness instead of Christ's power to

---

5 How I went about building my faith in His promises is explained in Appendix C of *Putting On The Armor of God*. Also included there is a listing of about 900 powerful and life-changing promises, which the reader could use to start his own arsenal of faith-building spiritual weapons. For additional helps on building faith by claiming God's promises, see Chapter Eight in *Great Shall Be Your Joy* (pp. 100-105) and pp. 129 – 133 in part two of *In The Arms of His Love*.

remove that sinfulness, I had prevented myself from obtaining the faith I needed and foolishly perpetuated the very thing I was trying to stop.

With no computer or scripture software, I used printed concordances to compile and analyze over two thousand references which testify that Jesus Christ is a God of power, love, kindness, patience, and mercy. Using nothing but a plain old typewriter, I copied these verses onto 3X5 cards which I could then carry with me and review through the day. Some of my favorites are:

> "He has all power to save every man that believeth on his name and bringeth forth fruit meet for repentance" (Alma 12:15).

> And Ammon's powerful testimony: "I know that I am nothing; as to my strength I am weak; therefore I will not boast of myself, but I will boast of my God, *for in his strength I can do all things . . .*" (Alma 26:12).

> Also, "He giveth power to the faint; and to them that have no might he increaseth strength" (Isaiah 40:29).

> "And Christ hath said: If ye will have faith in me ye shall have power to do whatsoever thing is expedient in me" (Moroni 7:33).

All those verses that I collected testified that Christ would gladly share with us all that is required to change our fallen natures from the vacillation of the "natural man" to a strong man of God. They testify that through surrendering to Him and trusting His will, we can be changed from what we are to what He would have us be. They testify that He came to rescue us from our sins, not to sit idly by, waiting until we have somehow cleansed and delivered ourselves; that He is truly "the way" out of our sins, and that He is indeed, the *only* way back to the Father.

I had been so ignorant of the Savior's grace, and so blind to His love and power and interest in me that such a study was invaluable in building my faith and confidence to reach out to Him. As my faith in the Savior grew, I was able to feel the Father's love and concern for me. The more that I learned of Them, the more astonished I became. I was embarking on a wonderfully exciting adventure! How amazing it was to learn that all this had been right there, available to me all that time.[6]

---

6 For additional explanations of this divine source of power, see Appendix C in this book, as well as Chapters 1, 5, 12 and 13 in *Great Shall Be Your Joy*, which discuss His grace, sharing in His power and building a sure foundation on Christ that will lead us into true righteousness. Also, see Chapter Four in *Conquering Your Own Goliaths*.

Whereas I had spent my life relying only upon my own strength to change, I now fell in love with instructions such as the following:

> The greatest and most important of all requirements of our Father in Heaven and of his Son Jesus Christ . . . is to believe in Jesus Christ, confess him, seek to know him, cling to him, make friends with him. Take a course to open a communication with your Elder Brother or file-leader—our Savior [Brigham Young, *Journal of Discourses*, Vol. 8, p. 339. Also quoted in 1982 *Relief Society Manual*, Salt Lake City, Utah: the Church of Jesus Christ of Latter-day Saints, p. 25].

> We function best in an environment of freedom. We are free when we are independent, and we are totally independent only when we are completely dependent upon the Savior [Hugh W. Pinnock, *Devotional Speeches of the Year*, Provo, Utah: Brigham Young University Press, 1979, p. 116].

HE WILL RAISE UP HELPERS

We may think we are alone in our struggles, but I testify that the moment we are capable of receiving help, God will raise up someone to help us find the path back to Him. It may be in the form of friends, books, articles or talks, or perhaps even a song we hear. I have personally experienced help from each of these channels.

Because of my moral transgressions, I had felt inferior, hollow, and hypocritical all of my life, and so I kept everyone at a distance. Consequently, I had never made even one close friend. The friend the Lord brought into my life at this time worked in the church seminary program and also as a professional therapist. Out of all the counselors I might have met, this man was the perfect friend for me, a man who was willing to frame his counseling in the scriptural terms that I needed to get past my doubts and hang-ups.

For example, in spite of all I was learning, I could not believe that God actually loved me. Not after all I had done, not after all my broken promises and covenants. With my intellect I knew that God must love me. He had to because "God is love." But the only love I had ever understood was conditional love, offered when worthy, withdrawn when unworthy. Knowing I was completely unworthy of God's love, my heart simply could not conceive of a love so great that it could reach past my faults to care about me anyway.

So Charlie's friendship was invaluable because he befriended me with an unconditional love, a love without criticism or judgment for what I had done or for what I had become. And, like the Lord, he believed I could change. My friend spent time with me when I needed to talk. I could call him anytime of the day or night. I could tell him anything—my fears, my worries and doubts, my sins. Along with the scriptures I was learning, my friend helped me to discover and trust in the Lord's unwavering love for me. (I emphasize this part of my rescue in the hope that every excommunicant will find a kind home teacher, a priesthood leader, or someone who will care enough to stick with him for as long as it takes to work his way back. Nothing is as powerful or healing as love!)

He also taught me from the scriptures that we have no right to judge, condemn or punish ourselves for our sins or weaknesses. This was a really tough lesson for me because I had not only become an expert in that, I thought it was my duty! But he convinced me, through the scriptures, that judgment and punishment belong to God, not to man. Together we discovered that I had actually allowed my feelings of guilt to become a form of self-punishment for my cycles of sin. He helped me recognize that in a perverted sort of way, I was substituting self-imposed misery for true repentance and that I had to let go of that awful habit.

I also learned from him that letting go of our grudges, bitterness and malice, particularly that which we feel toward ourselves, is a necessary part of placing our faith in the Savior's Atonement. The Savior cannot fix today if all we think about is yesterday. He showed me how King Benjamin's converts expressed their faith in the Savior by specifically asking God to "*apply*" the merits of the Savior's blood on their behalf.

> And they had viewed themselves in their own carnal state, even less than the dust of the earth. And they all cried aloud with one voice, saying: *O have mercy, and apply the atoning blood of Christ that we may receive forgiveness of our sins, and our hearts may be purified*; for we believe in Jesus Christ, the Son of God . . . [Mosiah 4:2].

Could His redemption actually be had for the asking? I was beginning to realize that it certainly would never be found without asking!

IN SUMMARY

On the cross, our Savior declared: "It is finished!" This was an announcement that the Atonement was now fully prepared and ready for man's release from all parts of the fallen human condition. The work of the Atonement is not "finished," however, until it is accepted in our own hearts and then honored through a lifetime of obedience and enduring to the end, all made possible by His grace and strength and partnership.

I do not have the words to describe the intensity of the love and gratitude which I now feel for my Savior, and which I have received from Him and Heavenly Father. Their divine and stubborn love simply cannot be reduced to the confinement of mortal words. In Ephesians 3:19, Paul said that Their love "passeth *knowledge*," but thankfully, it does not have to pass the understanding and perception of personal experience, which is the only way we can ever begin to conceive of Their infinite love for us.

The Lord changed my life from despair to ecstasy, from lust to love and from helplessness to victory. The Savior's intervention in my life was an act of total mercy, for I had absolutely no merit with which to claim His blessings. He did it for me and I know that He will do it for anyone so that we may share with Him the love and fellowship He enjoys with the Father.

CHAPTER THIRTEEN

TEMPLE BLESSINGS

Before an excommunicated person can be rebaptized, he must appear before a disciplinary council, preferably of the same stake high council or bishopric, for review of his or her progress. These men must be satisfied by the evidence presented, and by inspiration, that the person has truly repented and has become worthy of rebaptism. After I was healed of my sexual addictions and had improved the relationships with my family, and most importantly, once I had an inner conviction of God's forgiveness, I requested an appointment with our stake president to request the reconvening of the council. Once the appointment was made, there were several weeks to wait. During this waiting period, we made it a matter of family prayer that the stake president's response to the interview would be favorable.

On the evening of the interview our family had a wonderful spiritual experience. After a period of fasting, LoAnne and I gathered the family together and had a discussion about repentance and making amends, about paying the required price for our mistakes and about forgiveness. We emphasized the truth that God is in charge and guides the decisions of our leaders. We emphasized that only Heavenly Father knew if my heart was totally right. Only He could judge whether it was time for me to come back into the Church. We explained to the children that God would inspire the stake president to make the right decision, and we must be prepared to accept a "not yet," if that was his feeling. Each member of the family agreed with us that as much as we all wanted the baptism, even more than that we must want to be in harmony with God's will. Then we knelt in a circle holding hands, and each took a turn in prayer. The thrust of each prayer was gratitude for my healing, gratitude for our family, and to ask for the Spirit to inspire the president to make the proper decision in my behalf. There were tears shining on our faces at the conclusion of our prayer and our hearts were warm and confident that God would be a real part of this important interview. What a moving experience it was to hear and feel the intense depth of desire each child expressed to have me back in the Church with them.

This would be my first interview and report to the stake president since my excommunication, but there was no fear or concern in my heart as I approached his home. I felt completely calm and confident. I knew that my old man of sin had been crucified and that I had been made a new creature in Christ through the refining fires of adversity. Even though I had not yet been baptized and pronounced clean, I felt clean because I had a personal witness that I was now acceptable to the Lord. If there were some reason the stake president felt the need to say, "No, not yet," I could accept his decision and wait for as long as was needed, knowing that I was now right with God.

I expressed those feelings in my interview. I told him of my conversion, how Christ had rescued me from the sexual addictions and of the things I had discovered about the doctrine of Christ. I explained my new understanding of the Atonement, which I had previously taken for granted. I told him of our family unity and how blessed I felt that my family had stood with me through all the anguish.

It was obvious, at the beginning of the interview, that he was very reserved and cautious about reconvening a court. He confided to me that he had once allowed the rebaptism of a person too soon, and it had broken his heart to see the transgression repeated, with all the resulting penalties and heartaches. His caution was obvious, both from his questions and his posture. That was okay. I didn't blame him. Coming back into the Church is not a light matter. It is an extremely important decision because the Lord has warned of even more severe penalties if the transgression is repeated. (See D&C 82:7). He will not be mocked! I appreciated the caution and care manifested by my stake president as his careful questions, guided by the Spirit, directed the interview into an examination of my heart, my testimony, and my commitments. As his questions continued, and as the Spirit filled the room, there came a visible point in the interview at which he smiled and relaxed. He had received what he needed as my judge—the witness of the Spirit. I came away grateful that it was not an easy interview.

Before the stake president would make any final decision about reconvening a full council, however, he wanted a chance to interview my wife. He felt he could learn much about me from her feelings.

Surely, this was a wise decision, but it was hard to endure the waiting as her interview was scheduled a few days later. When the time came she, too, came away from his kind and gentle interview with the feeling that it had been guided by the Spirit. He would only say to her, as he had said to me, that he would make it a matter of earnest prayer.

As we waited for his decision, we expressed our gratitude to the Lord for His guidance and continued our pleas for a positive response. We also prayed for the strength to accept the answer if it should be negative. How excited and thrilled we were, a short time later, to receive a letter from him as official notification that the high council court would be convened, giving date, time and place, and requesting our attendance there.

I have already related the care and cautious concern with which the original court deliberated their verdict. The same care was taken this time. Both my bishop and my wife had been requested to provide the court with written statements of testimony concerning my conversion and their feelings about my possible rebaptism. The following is part of the testimony that LoAnne provided:

> Gerald is undeniably a changed man. This change is reflected in every aspect of his life, but I notice it particularly in our marriage relationship and in his relationships with our children. It is such an amazing change that it took me several months to comprehend that it was real and honest. Now I truly understand that when the Lord affects a healing, He heals the whole man from the inside out.[1]

> Whether or not the time is right for Gerald's rebaptism and acceptance into the Church, he is right with the Lord and we, his wife and children, are content to follow him and support him as we wait in patience for that time to arrive.

The reconvened council first reviewed the minutes of the original court, along with my bishop's letter and this letter from LoAnne. The stake president then expressed his feelings about his interviews with us. It was then time for me to speak to the brethren on my own behalf. That was much more difficult than I had expected it to be. I felt a powerful presence of the Lord's Spirit in the room. I felt the combined strength and love of those sixteen brethren, and I felt such an overwhelming gratitude to God for bringing me to this point that I could

---

1 Seeking total healing instead of merely stopping an inappropriate behavior is discussed in Chapter Two of *Draw Near Unto Me*, Steven A. Cramer.

hardly speak. My testimony was frequently interrupted by uncontrollable weeping, but this time, instead of bitter tears of remorse like I had shed at the first court, these were tears of gratitude and rejoicing. I expressed the feelings that were in my heart for the Lord and His Church and for my family. When the testimonies and questions were completed, we were excused. The brethren then counseled together to receive the Lord's will concerning me. Twenty-five minutes later, they called us back to give us the verdict: a unanimous agreement to recommend me for rebaptism. We received the following letter shortly thereafter:

> This is to formally notify you of the results of the high council court held in your behalf on this date. Since you were present, you are already aware that it was the decision of the court that we recommend to the First Presidency that approval be granted for your rebaptism.[2]

> We rejoice with you over this decision and are grateful for your courage and determination to overcome the problems that have confronted you. We recognize also that the love and support of a good wife and fine children have assisted you in your accomplishment.

> We will transmit the results of the court to the First Presidency and await their decision before the baptism can actually be performed. May the Lord bless you in your future endeavors.

How can I describe the feeling of relief and gratitude of having those brethren give official ratification to my personal feelings of repentance? What a wonderful blessing God has given to provide these formal ecclesiastical procedures of the Church to examine and confirm the changes which take place in our lives as we finally make our life right with the Lord.

Because Gerald was working nights, he usually got up around 9:00 P.M. to say goodnight to the family, eat, and prepare for work. One special evening about a month later he got up as usual, and sat down to eat. One by one, I sent each of our children to give him a kiss and a hug, and to say, "Congratulations, Dad." Not suspecting anything, he grew more and more curious with each child's performance. And then we told him the wonderful news: Our bishop had called during the day to say that permission had been granted for his rebaptism.

It didn't take long to make the arrangements. Friends and relatives

---

2 Such approval is not necessary in all cases.

dropped what they were doing and came to share my joy only four days later. When I was placed under the water, my impression was one of literally being buried, and it felt so good, knowing what was being buried there, that I wanted my body to just keep going down, deeper and deeper, placing my old man of sin forever beyond reach or view. All too soon I was lifted back in symbolism of the new birth which Christ had given me. That newness of life, that wonderful feeling of being whole and complete before Him, dimmed the awful memories of the past, making it possible to open my heart to His infinite love. Far more than a symbol, baptism is truly the doorway to a new life.

Following my baptism, I was allowed to participate in church functions the same as any new member who did not hold the priesthood. It was a great step forward to be a small part of the Church and to have the sacred privilege of serving the Master, even in a limited capacity. But most joyous of all, I could again partake of the sacrament with my family. The first Sunday after my rebaptism, my children—indeed the whole congregation—watched as I was offered and then partook of those sacred emblems. On that day in our ward, no one took this sacred ordinance for granted, and I noticed mine were not the only tears shed.

After a lengthy period of probation (which was measured in years, not weeks or months), application papers were sent to the First Presidency and nine months later, my request for the restoration of my priesthood and temple blessings was approved by the prophet subject to a final interview by a visiting general authority.

Included in Gerald's application were letters from our bishop and stake president, from Gerald and me, and from each of our older children. It is instructive to read our children's letters for they poignantly illustrate that experiences such as ours involve the entire family, not just the excommunicant, or even just the excommunicant and his wife. This is an example of the fact that there is no such thing as "private sin" within a family. The actions, attitudes and behavior of any one person in a household inescapably spills over into the lives of all the family members, whether for good or bad. I cannot read these letters without weeping.

FROM TRACY, AGE FIFTEEN:

Dear President Kimball,

"The gospel means a lot to me, and it is a very important thing in my life. In fact, it is the most important thing to me other than my family. About ____ years ago, when my dad was excommunicated, it struck me very harshly. He knew it was true, he was just having problems and temptations, and as a result, he made some very bad mistakes. When I realized what he had done, I was totally shocked because I never believed that my dad, of all dads, would ever fall away from the church.

"President Kimball, a couple of years ago were the worst years I have ever lived. I never knew we would all have to go through so much to pay the price of my dad's sins, and to get him away from Satan's clutches back into the gospel. If only he had realized that Jesus already paid the price of his sins, and all he had to do was turn his life over to Jesus. Well, my dad didn't realize this at the time, and I never knew that either.

"I never once got upset with Jesus or Heavenly Father for letting this happen to our family, but I have felt frustrated, because I thought they weren't answering my millions of thousands of truly sincere prayers. But now, as I look back, I can figure out how they did answer them. The change in my dad is incredible. He literally changed from darkness to light. My dad is literally a "new born" man. He is a different person that I love and respect. I promise that it is so good to be around him. Before, it was always scary to be by him because he'd always have a grouchy look on his face. And if you talked to him, he'd either not answer, or practically bite your head off with his rude and nasty replies. Now he is pleasant to be around. I don't know how to explain it, but when you're around him, you get a special feeling, like you can tell he is so righteous. Now his face is always bright and smiling.

"Not only has my dad's life changed, but mine has also, as a result. Because of my dad, I now know that I can actually have a real relationship with Christ. I can be a true friend, and he can be a friend to me. Jesus saved my dad, and I'll be eternally grateful to Him for that."

FROM OUR OLDEST DAUGHTER, JERI ANN, AGE TWENTY:

Dear President Kimball,

"I thank you for taking time out of your busy day to read my letter. It means so much to me and my family. My father was excommunicated a few years ago. He had a very hard struggle trying to make himself become worthy again, but that was what his problem was. You see, for forty years, he had been trying to do everything himself, to become good enough for God. Then one day, the Lord showed him what his problem was. My father finally saw how proud he was to think he could make it on his own.

"Next, he set out to search the scriptures to learn all about the grace of God. He looked up every scripture on grace, but he couldn't understand them. So God told him he needed to understand His power in order to understand His grace. So he looked up every scripture on power. This study went on until my dad knew all about eighteen or so subjects. Then he went back to the scriptures on grace and he understood them all.[3]

"Well, it didn't take long till he was ready to be rebaptized. Let me tell you that he is a different person now. Jesus Christ is his best friend. He and my mother no longer have serious problems in their marriage. I feel that he is now ready to have his priesthood and temple blessings restored. Our family is lacking only in being sealed to Dad for eternity.

"President Kimball, I know that this is God's true church, and that you are called by Him to be His prophet today. I know that He will tell you whether my father is worthy now or not. I feel that he is, but I have complete faith that you will make the right decision whether my dad can now have his priesthood restored or if we will have to wait a little longer."

FROM DON, OUR OLDEST SON, AGE TWENTY-ONE:

Dear President Kimball,

"It is with great pleasure that I am writing this note of my feelings about my father. I am on a mission, and I have really enjoyed serving the Lord here for the past two years. I soon will be home again with my family. I'm really looking forward to meeting my baby sister, Kristy, who was born a little over a year ago when I'd already been in Brazil a few months. But I'm looking forward even more to meet my father, who was also born—born again—during my mission. To me, it will truly be like meeting a new person.

"My father was excommunicated about a year and a half before I

---

3   The results of that study are provided in my second book, *Great Shall Be Your Joy*. It includes chapters on God's desire to share His grace and power with us, how to overcome our natural-man pride, become submissive and trusting in God's promises to us, and how to develop a Christ-centered foundation that will lead us into true righteousness and spiritual victory.

began my mission. Between his excommunication and my mission, I often had long, personal talks with Dad. He'd tell me how he was feeling and what he thought were his real problems. I could see he was feeling more and more discouraged and hopeless. Dad even told me several times of thoughts of suicide, or of at least leaving the family. Though I was young and inexperienced, I loved him and I tried the best I could to give him advice and encouragement, but I'm afraid I wasn't of much help. It was difficult for me to understand what he was going through, but I could tell he was getting worse, not better.

"When I entered the MTC and began receiving letters from home, I began to see a difference in Dad. He was beginning to realize he didn't have to make it on his own, for the Savior was there to help him and to really become his personal Redeemer. Miracle after miracle occurred, and every letter I received was filled with more enthusiasm and more examples of concepts the Savior had helped Dad to learn. Not just my father's letters, but also the letters from my mother, brother and sisters were all full of marvelings at what a change was being wrought in Dad's heart. It wasn't very many months before he had, through the Savior, overcome all his problems. Now I wasn't there to personally witness the change that occurred, but maybe being farther removed helped me see even clearer the drastic change of attitudes.

"It was interesting to me that quite shortly after Dad had said he'd overcome his problems, I began receiving letters telling of how he was trying to help others overcome their problems. Since Dad's rebirth, I've been amazed at all he's done in his effort to share the Savior with all he comes in contact with. Before Dad's excommunication, I never saw him so interested in helping others as he is now. Now the only thing he seems to be interested in is helping others to come to know the Savior as he has. I can't wait to get home so Dad can help me to further develop my relationship with the Lord."

FROM JANAE, AGE EIGHTEEN:

Dear President Kimball,

"Before Dad was excommunicated, we hardly saw him at all. I never got to be with him or get to know him at all. Dad would never have very much to say and he would be so serious. It was a very rare thing to see him smiling and as things progressed on, he would get really crabby and very impatient. It was hard to understand. I still loved him a great deal and wanted so bad to be able to talk to him like I could with Mom.

"Then after arriving home from a meeting one night, Mom and Dad sat down with the older kids and told us about his excommunication. I felt so bad. I didn't know the full meaning of it, though. I hugged Dad and told him I forgave him. I hoped so bad that he'd repent and want to get back on the right track. I had so much faith in him and prayed for him every night and morning.

"We were so happy when he was rebaptized ____ years later. Since then, he's been with us a lot more and has made it a point to do things with us. It seems that Dad is just a totally new and different person now that he has found how to be close to the Savior. I think it is wonderful. I can talk to Dad a lot easier now, though I'm still not used to it. Dad has tons more patience now than he did all put together in that period of time. My respect and love for Dad grows all the time I am around him.

"Dad has studied very hard in the scriptures and has taught us kids quite a bit concerning them. We'd all get together on Sundays and read and study the scriptures. Dad would very patiently explain what we were talking about to the little kids. He would never have done that before. Dad is a very great example for me. He's endured many things which I never even knew about. And now he puts everything into a spiritual and eternal perspective. He teaches me so many things and he shows his love to others now. Thanks for taking time to read this. I hope this has helped you in some way. I trust your decision completely because I know it is the will of Heavenly Father."

FROM OUR SECOND SON, CHAD, AGE FOURTEEN:

Dear President Kimball,

"When I was first informed by my parents of my dad's excommunication, I was only ten and a half years of age and I didn't know how to handle the situation. The full force of it didn't hit me until a few months later. This is because he just gradually became worse and worse with his problem, and until about the third year of his excommunication, he never really did anything except grow worse with attitude and problems.

"I can recall being terrified because he would yell and argue about little things that didn't even matter. I remember hating to be around him because he was so unpleasant to be around, and he carried such a gross spirit with him that left you feeling sick. It stayed that way until about his third year of being excommunicated. I almost died whenever I had to see him suffer the way he did.

"It was about his third year when he finally began to pull out of it. He really got a good friend that understood him, loved him for what he was, and tried to help him anyway that he possibly could. We all were doing that same thing, but he just couldn't see that. For trying so hard I admired him more than anybody else in the world. For doing what he did to eventually get his blessings restored to him and reseal the family together for all time and eternity, I loved him.

"Now he has suffered for so long that it seems that the price to pay was more than what any of us expected, but we never would have made it this far if we hadn't stuck together and always tried our very best to be a forever family. If we had even once slipped and if even one of us gave up the fight to help our dad and ourselves, we definitely would not be in the blessed situation that we are in right now.

"I could never put on paper or even into words of my own how I feel for my dad. All I can really say is that it only takes a mere man to be a father, but it takes a really special man to be a dad. I feel there is not a single man in the world with as much love for me as this man has, and I wouldn't give him up for the world."

Frequently, in situations such as this, the children will use the mistakes of a wayward parent to justify their own rebellion. None of our children chose that path. Since then, five of our nine children have served missions. All of them have been endowed and are faithful to their temple covenants. The eight who have married did so in the temple and are raising our grandchildren to be obedient and to love the Lord.

The next time a General Authority came to our area for a stake conference, I met with him for final clearance. After his careful and lengthy interview, he placed his hands upon my head. As he said the words: "In the name of our Lord, Jesus Christ," an expression so sacred, so long anticipated, I felt grateful to know that he not only had the authority to use them, but was actually speaking on behalf of my personal Friend. He pronounced me clean and restored each priesthood and temple blessing individually. What an incredible thrill we experienced as LoAnne and I embraced following that beautiful ordinance. At last we could become an eternal family again!

The next day brought a great surprise. I felt so different that I was astonished. It was almost as if I were another person. I felt whole, completed. Until my blessings were restored, I hadn't realized how accustomed I had grown to the feelings of incompleteness, without the temple or the priesthood in my life. That same week LoAnne and I went through the temple together for the first time in many years. As I once again reverently placed the holy temple garment upon my body, it felt as though the Lord, Himself, were putting His loving arms around me. I felt safe, secure, protected and accepted. What words can describe the feelings of being whole, of belonging and knowing that you are accepted? I can only say that it is worth any sacrifice that is required.

As quickly as possible we obtained temple recommends for each of our children who had been baptized. Then, except for our eldest son who was away at school, the whole family went to the temple to have Kristy, our little daughter who had been born just prior to Gerald's rebaptism, sealed to us. It was an inspiring experience to have our children surround us in the temple, each one dressed in white, looking like a small company of angels. As my husband and I knelt at the altar, our little girl beside us with her tiny hand on ours, we received the glorious sealing promise that would make our family eternally complete.

Following that ordinance, we all stood where the children could see their images reflected endlessly in the mirrors, and they all promised to live worthily and to come back to the temple for their own eternal blessings. Today we are grateful that they have all done so and are faithful to their covenants.

As enormously rewarding and satisfying as these experiences were to me, the major emotion that I felt was not one of personal satisfaction for what I had received, but a tremendous sense of gratitude to the Lord for helping me give back to my family that which I had so cruelly taken from them years before. Yet, now it was real and eternal and truly appreciated.

CHAPTER 14

THE DEPRESSION YEARS

As difficult as the buffeting years were, we didn't realize until much later the toll they had taken on Gerald's health—more particularly, his mental health. It was only weeks after the change of nature he received that he plunged into a fit of negativity and depression. It seemed amazing, because we both knew he'd changed, that he now had control over his temptations, that he was on track to know and understand the Savior in ways never before imagined. Yet, he continued to struggle with his emotions and with negative feelings.

At the same time, I was losing control over my emotions as a result of his continued attacks against me, and the withdrawal of the Lord's endowment of grace. Because I began to struggle with depression, I went to a fireside presentation titled, "Depression and the Mormon Woman," given by an LDS psychologist. This was the first time I had opportunity to understand that depression is a valid mental and emotional illness and that it may require professional help and medication to deal with it. But, as its symptoms were described, I found that, instead of describing my feelings and state of mind, he was describing Gerald's! Gerald could have been his model of the manic-depressive patient!

Because his symptoms were so clearly explained, I felt encouraged that, perhaps, something medical could be done to help him. Yet, when I questioned the cost of such treatment afterwards, I was dismayed to discover it was high, far beyond our means. It seemed that only the rich could afford the counseling and medications that would be needed to deal with that condition. I hoped a way could be provided for us, but didn't ever imagine that it would. However, the very next week, three things happened that gave us the opportunity to seek professional help. Money we had sent to Gerald's parents on a mission was sent back with a note that it was no longer needed. Friends in the Church approached me and asked if they could, without Gerald's knowing, give us money for such treatment. (I do not believe I had even spoken of this need to them!) And our bishop decided professional help was needed and made an appointment with Church social services for Gerald. Three answers were provided simultaneously to help us fill our need! It seemed obvious to me that the Lord still cared very much for our family and was assisting us to obtain help for Gerald.

The following entry is from my journal after his first appointments with the psychologist (for counseling) and the psychiatrist (for medication):

14 March   Gerald has been started on an anti-depressant and will be meeting regularly with a wonderful counselor. On the way home from these appointments, I felt strongly that we were doing the right thing and that it was now out of my hands and into the hands of someone who can really help Gerald. The feeling was so strong and pervasive that I felt an almost tangible relief. It was as though a huge, heavy load had been removed from me and as if the Lord said to me (and I could almost hear the words), "You've done enough and well. Now relax and see my power made manifest in his behalf." And the relief was so great it cannot be described.

There is no question that the Lord guided us into this solution step by step. It was only six months later that Gerald was able to stop counseling. His whole attitude had been reshaped. To me it seemed as though the Lord had entered his very person, cleaned his "house," discarded all the debris of past attitudes and false desires and left him with a glowing feeling of forgiveness and love which was evident in his demeanor. It was a miracle.

I became pregnant during this time and suffered through a difficult pregnancy. I was a few days short of forty years old when our last child was born, a beautiful little daughter. Kristy was the reason, two years later after his blessings were restored, that we took our children to the temple to have her sealed to us.

If the story could end there, it would be a "happily ever after" ending. But life is not like that. Instead, our Heavenly Father has provided that our lives are built upon one challenge after another, and until our life ends, we will face struggle and testing that is designed to make us humble ourselves and become more like Him, that we may eventually be where He is.

THE CRUSADE

Because of the tremendous change Gerald had experienced, he had a driving need to offer what he had learned to others who might need that hope. In addition, the General Authority who had given him the ordinance that restored his temple blessings had told us he felt inspired that Gerald should write a book about his experiences. With that encouragement, Gerald wrote his first book, The Worth of a Soul. *During the next twenty years, he was contacted by hundreds of people who had been or were suffering as he had and who took great encouragement from the support Gerald could give them.[1] He also authored six more books that more fully explained the principles behind his change of nature and being freed from Satan's power. He was invited to speak at countless firesides, both at home and all across the United States.*

He poured his whole self into this crusade and simply could not understand why I would not do likewise. I had a family that still needed the bulk of my attention, and I still felt rooted to the person I was. On the other hand, he was anxious to give up all he had been and to "take up the cross," so to speak, and carry its banner into the lives of all who would listen. This, at times, became a point of contention between us until Gerald learned that he could not entirely give up his old identity. It was a struggle for him, and he again sought out his old friend and former counselor who helped him with this difficult transition.

It should also be noted that, for many people, depression medications do not last in their beneficial effect upon the body. After a time, the body becomes resistant to them and their effectiveness is lost. It is a gradual process, but eventually one understands that something has gone horribly wrong and he must seek out the physician and receive a prescription for another, different medication that will help in like manner. There are also side effects that must be dealt with, and sometimes, medication for those side effects that must also be prescribed. Medication is not a magic solution, nor a permanent one.

Each time the medication wore off, the old depressions and manic attitudes came rushing back into our lives. Again, we had to contend with false assumptions and accusations and marital discord as these things took over in Gerald's brain.

AS REMEMBERED BY GERALD

As the months and years passed, we were not living "happily ever after." In fact, as time progressed, life was rapidly getting worse and worse. I was miserable and so was our marriage. It was extremely confusing. With my depressed thinking, I reasoned that Christ had healed me and I had been happy for the first time in my life, but now I was miserable. Since I had not returned to sin, there *had* to be another cause—I needed something or someone to blame. Well, it must be the

---

1 Many of those requests concerned issues that are common to all of us. Much of this had been recorded in Steven's book, *Conquering Your Own Goliaths.*

marriage. As stupid as this sounds, I found myself blaming it all on my wife.

Always on the alert for such an opportunity, the devil now rushed to attack our marriage. He whispered constant lies about how awful and unreasonable my wife had become, how my misery was all her fault, and how, now that I was a better person, I deserved a better companion. I still had not learned how susceptible I could be to the demons who were planting these thoughts into my mind, so once again I fell victim to their lies. In the twisted and flawed thinking of my chemically depressed brain, I felt certain that it was all true. I was totally naïve and uninformed about the increased trouble and complexities caused by divorce, even when it is justified. In my confusion and misery, that seemed the only logical solution.

Once, during a walk in a pine forest, as I meditated, prayed and sang hymns, I was feeling very close to my Heavenly Father. Then, as I bent over, to pass under a low branch, I saw a snake curled around the branch, hissing and ready to strike. This unexpected encounter frightened me and spoiled the mood. At the time, I was angered by the intrusion, but I have come to appreciate that experience, because for me, it is a symbol of Satan, always lurking where we least expect him, always ready to strike and poison our lives.

I think misery will always seek an escape that appears to be the quickest and easiest. But even in that frame of mind, after coming out of decades where LoAnne had been supportive, patient and forgiving, divorce was not an easy thing to think about. After all she had done to help the Lord save me, it seemed unthinkable to leave her now. And with nine children rejoicing over my rescue, how could I now devastate them with a divorce? They were huge questions, but each time we had an unresolved disagreement, that same answer pounded in my brain as an escape.[2]

I became so convinced that divorce was the solution, I began campaigning among our grown children. I reasoned that if they agreed with me how awful she was and supported me in the idea of leaving, it would somehow work out okay. I do not recall what it was that I told them that could have undone her years of righteous, faithful service to them and holding of the family together in spite of my problems, but I must have been convincing, because I soon had some of them agreeing with me.

---

2 For further discussion on divorce, see Appendix A.

To go to the children like that, behind her back, poisoning their opinion of their mother, without her having an opportunity to defend herself was a vicious and cruel thing to have done. As horrible as all those years of sexual immorality and betrayal to our marriage vows were, I consider this divorce campaign to have been an equally, if not even more cruel and terrible thing to have done. It seems a miracle to me that this elect woman survived this new crisis and continued to forgive and wait patiently for the day the Lord would heal the marriage as he had my addictions. I will be eternally indebted to her.

Eventually I discovered that there are all-natural nutritional supplements that, for many people, can be just as effective as the chemical prescriptions. With the encouragement and guidance of a doctor, I replaced the prescription medication with natural supplements and received yet another miraculous birth-like experience.[3]

Once those chemicals were cleared from my system, and once I learned to balance the depression with food supplementation, life felt like Christmas again. To my surprise, I discovered that I had been living numb for seventeen years. While the medications had protected me from the plunges into negativity and hostility, they had also prevented me from experiencing normal feelings of joy and happiness. It was like coming out of a trance. At last the way was prepared for the Lord to work yet another miracle in our lives.

SAVED BY A MISSION

The lowest point in our relationship occurred at the same time that Wendi, our seventh child who had been studying at BYU, went on a mission. She was full of faith and the fire of the gospel and served a valiant, enthusiastic mission for the Lord. However, at home, things had degenerated to the point that I was, finally, ready to give up the fight and consent to a divorce from Gerald. I had come to the conclusion, which he readily verified, that our love was dead and he no longer cared to be married to me.

Wendi, however, wrote home about the sorrow she felt for one of her companions whose parents had divorced while she was on her mission and what a heartache that was for her companion to bear. Then Wendi said, "I am so thankful that I don't have to worry about that." I decided that our divorce could wait at least until she got home from her mission.

---

3 For more information on depression, please see Appendix G.

By this time, all our children except Kristy, the youngest, now a teenager, had married or were working away from home. I no longer had a large family at home for which to bury my hurts or from which to draw the love I needed. Both Gerald and I had learned to draw within ourselves and to seek satisfaction in human relationships from other sources.

Also during the time Wendi was on her mission, circumstances worked out that we could move to another state. The excitement of the move, a new job, integrating ourselves into a new church environment, new callings, and getting Kristy into a new school involved our interest and diverted our attention from the need for a divorce. Our marriage relationship was empty, completely unfulfilling; however, bitterness was controlled and we had a mostly amicable relationship. We were almost like two casual friends living in the same house, but only occasionally interacting with each other.

By the time Wendi returned from her mission, we had learned to live with a measure of peace in this condition. Gerald had found a natural food product that would treat his depression better, without side effects, and without losing its effectiveness. That find was also an obvious blessing from the Lord, miraculous in its discovery following a priesthood blessing.

We never brought it up, but the knowledge I had that Gerald did not love me gnawed at me and, were it not for the love I felt from my Heavenly Father and my children, I would have been devastated, indeed. It seemed to me that no earthly power, no amount of good intentions, no ability to endure, could ever resurrect a loving relationship from the dead ashes of our marriage. I concluded that, if it were to be saved, it would take an act of God and most probably not until the next life.

I felt very low in spirit, but had re-determined to endure to the end, hoping for a better life after my death. I went to my new bishop and asked for a blessing. There was no way I could describe to him all that had occurred in our lives and all the reasons for my low spiritedness. I told him so, and asked that he would just give me a blessing and let the Lord, who knew everything, tell me what I must do, hoping I would be strengthened for the long endurance time left in my life.

To my surprise, the bishop was willing to do that. He laid his hands on my head, and in tones of gentleness expressed my Heavenly Father's love for me. He reassured me as to the correctness of my life and promised me that I would find all I seek if I would turn again to the scriptures and be more diligent in reading from the Book of Mormon every day. It seemed unbelievable to me, but I took the Lord up on his words. As I read daily from that sacred record, I found a new sense of peace and love flooding into my life. It was as if the Lord wrapped His arms of love around me and assured me that all was well, that He was aware of me and would sustain me. It was just the lift I needed, and it also prepared me for the inspiration that was to come.

General conference has always been a time of renewal and refreshment for me. This one was no different. However, as I sat alone in our living room and watched, one of the messages was born into my heart in a particular way. The speaker wasn't even talking about senior couples serving missions, but what he said allowed the Holy Spirit to whisper to me that Gerald and I should serve a mission together. It was an astounding thought! Was it really possible??

Later that week Gerald and I drove to the mountains to a secluded spot and talked about the possibility. Finances were tight and seemed prohibitive. We brainstormed all possible alternatives, but finally shelved it until something might change to allow such a thing to happen. Unbeknownst to us, a couple of months before, when Wendi was married and all the family were together for the occasion, our children had gotten together and talked about the possibility of sending us, their parents, on a mission. Our oldest son had obtained pledges of support from each of our children, but had thought the time was not yet right to mention it to us.

Our youngest daughter, Kristy, was to be married in just a few weeks. Gerald was to the point that he could retire from his job. I was also working, but had taken a leave of absence to help in the arrangements for Kristy's wedding. One of our other daughters happened to mention to me what they had previously discussed and decided. It all clicked. With their help, I knew we could serve a mission and that the Lord wanted us to do so at this time. It was crazy. We must have been out of our minds to think a marriage such as ours could survive a mission. After the parallel lives we had been living, it was incredible that we would risk being together twenty-four hours a day! But it was inspired and I knew it was right.

We submitted our papers, received our call and reported to the Senior Missionary Training Center—all within less than two months! During our nine week stay in Provo, as we struggled to learn a new language, we were immersed in the scriptures, imbued with the excitement of a new adventure, and in countless ways exposed to a daily infusion of the Spirit of the Lord. We felt rejuvenated and eager to serve.

Our mission could be a book in and of itself. The things we learned, the people we served and grew to love, the spiritual experiences, and the other missionaries who blessed us—all these things combined to add a marvelous chapter to our lives that can only be hinted at here. But on our mission, we learned this great and important truth: If we would act and speak in a manner that the

Holy Spirit could be invited into our companionship, we had a partnership with God that would erase the hurt and open our hearts to each other in ways we had never, ever experienced before. For the first time, we discovered what it was like to "be one." We learned the inestimable worth of having "His Spirit to be with us," as we make covenants each time we partake of the sacrament. How blessed was our reward for serving this mission together!

When my great-grandmother was in distress over a blessing she had been robbed of by ignorance and Satan's teachings, she sought an interview with the prophet for strength and comfort. Brigham Young told her on that occasion, "Whatever Satan has taken from you, the Lord can restore; but it will take great sacrifice on your part." I believe that with all my heart. My great-grandmother was willing to make the sacrifice Brigham Young required of her, and she received a hundred-fold blessing for it. Gerald and I—and our children—made the sacrifice of serving a mission for the Lord at the time He required it, and we also received a hundred-fold blessing. That which I had supposed would have to wait for another life in the next world, has been given to us now. That which Satan had deprived us of by all the years of addiction, depression and suffering, was restored, one hundred fold, by the Lord.

This, also, could be a "happily ever after" ending to our story. But we are still living in this mortal world, and so we must still continue to meet challenges and to grow. I do not know what is in store for us in the years remaining in our lives, but I am sure it will continue to challenge us and to bring us closer to Christ. However, I am so very grateful that, whatever it is, we will meet it together, as one, and with God's help, we will triumph.

EPILOGUE

We have completed our story. There is but one more thing to do, and that is to express our total assurance that no matter who you are, no matter what you have done, or even what you are still doing, the Lord loves you! He wants you!

From time to time we all live beneath who we *should* be, who we *want* to be and *could* be. We testify that it does not matter how long our sorrows have weighed us down; it does not matter how deep our transgressions have been; nor does it matter how deep our despair is; if we will humbly and sincerely come to God in a repentant attitude, there is hope.

I once hiked through the forest for over an hour, marveling at the beauty of God's creations and rejoicing to be there where I could soak it in. I then made my way through a ravine and up a hill. When I crested the hill I caught my breath at the view of the brilliant fall colors, bright yellows and reds in so many varieties, glowing perfectly in the afternoon sunlight.

Down the valley before me and rising on the next rolling hill was a carpet of trees, two huge stands of dark green pines, separated by the brilliant yellow of Aspens in their fall splendor. What a stunning contrast. To me it seemed an act of God's love, painted just for me. Looking beyond that hill, I could see row after row of rolling hills, similarly colored, stretching perhaps twenty miles to the horizon. It was staggering to contemplate the endless number of similar scenes that must cover the globe we live on. One could not drink it in with a glance. I found a rock and sat for perhaps an hour, trying to memorize the splendor.

As I sat there, I thought that I could be the very first man to ever visit here and view this beauty. But, as I rose to leave, I glanced under a bush and was horrified to see two rusted pop cans. I almost felt violated. The sacredness of my experience had been polluted by the world. But then the Spirit whispered this message in the words of the Savior:

"There is nothing you can ever experience, there is nowhere you can go that I have not already been there before you. You can never suffer pain, guilt, or heartache that I have not already tasted and paid for. You may think your mistakes make you the first, or the worst in your shame and pain, but I have descended below it all. You will never be the first because I loved you enough to go into every place and into every experience first, to prepare a way for your deliverance." I left my sacred mountaintop thankful for the pop cans.[1]

We often stumble in darkness and repeated failure because we just aren't wise enough to know the way. But Christ knows the way perfectly. "O how great the holiness of our God! For he knoweth all things, and *there is not anything* save he knows it" (2 Nephi 9:20). This omniscient knowledge is used to prepare the exact resources needed for each person. "For he is the same yesterday, to-day, and forever; and *the way is prepared for all men* [every man and woman] from the foundation of the world, *if* it so be that they repent and come unto him" (1 Nephi 10:18).

The summary of our entire story and message is the testimony that God's answers to our prayers, His provision for our needs, are never restrained by the limitations of seemingly impossible circumstances, for "there is no restraint to the LORD to save by many or by few" (1 Samuel 14:6).[2] There is *no situation* we can be in from which Christ cannot deliver us, whether it is physical, mental, emotional or spiritual. Indeed, "He is able also to save them *to the uttermost* that come unto God by him," and "*He has all power* to save every man that believeth on his name and bringeth forth fruit meet for repentance" (Hebrews 7:25; Alma 12:15; also Philippians 3:21).

> Thus we may see that the Lord is merciful unto all who will, in the sincerity of their hearts, call upon his holy name. Yea, thus we see that *the gate of heaven is open unto all*, even to those who will believe on the name of Jesus Christ, who is the Son of God.
>
> Yea, we see that *whosoever will* may lay hold upon the word of God, which is quick and powerful, which shall divide asunder all the cunning and the snares and the wiles of the devil, and lead the man of Christ in a strait and narrow course across that everlasting

---

1 For a discussion of the scriptures that validate this personal experience, see Chapter Two, "Does The Savior Understand," in *Great Shall Be Your Joy*.

2 See Judges 7, where the Lord reduced an Israelite army from 32,000 men to only 300 soldiers to demonstrate this very point.

gulf of misery which is prepared to engulf the wicked—

And land their souls, yea, their immortal souls, at the right hand of God in the kingdom of heaven, to sit down with Abraham, and Isaac, and with Jacob, and with all our holy fathers, *to go no more out* (Helaman 3:27–30).

Gerald and LoAnne

SISTER TO SISTER

I have come to understand that the terrible plague of pornography (which actually was only in its beginnings when Gerald was addicted) has mushroomed and is affecting Latter-day Saint families in epidemic proportions. It has gone from being a disease that needed to be courted to be caught to an onrushing plague that will infect all who do not take serious measures to avoid it. Its perpetrators have become expert at invading every home that has television or Internet access. Chatrooms become a conduit to its evils; interactive games reach out to the unsuspecting and draw them into its net. Commercial and cable TV advertise it, promote it and make it almost inescapable for every human being in our society.

It is naïve to suppose that Latter-day Saints are immune. The numerous letters we have received attest to the devastating effects in the marriages and families of many of the elect among us. Wives have been emotionally stabbed as their husbands have fallen into pornography and infidelity.[1] As Jacob testified to the priesthood holders of his day, "...Ye have broken the hearts of your tender wives, and lost the confidence of your children, because of your bad examples before them; and the sobbings of their hearts ascend up to God against you. And... many hearts died, pierced with deep wounds" (Jacob 2:35).

The purpose of this section is to address some of the concerns and questions that have come to us as a result of the first publication of The Worth of a Soul, and to encourage distressed wives and mothers whose loved ones have been victimized by Satan and by his pernicious programs of pornography and visual promiscuity.

A LETTER TO WIVES

You are a person of great worth. But when your mate chooses to find pleasure or satisfaction in something or someone outside the marriage relationship, it

---

1 For another first-person account, see an excellent article, "Breaking the Chains of Pornography," in February 2001 *Ensign*, pp. 54-59.

is a terrible rejection. It batters at the very foundations of self-esteem. His lust for pornography has nothing to do with the real you—or the real him. Realize that those "pleasures" are inspired by Satan and that they are completely apart from you and from your worth as an individual. It is something else apart. Don't be fooled into thinking there must be something wrong with you or that you are to blame.

It would be a beneficial exercise to begin every day by repeating the Relief Society declaration of women's worth. Think about it. You know He loves you and cares about the trials and tribulations you are suffering through no fault of your own. You know He will reach out and help you and calm your troubled soul when you need Him. These things you know, but it is easy to forget when we are assailed by doubts and by the false impressions given by a spouse's attraction to celluloid images of other women. Keep that Relief Society declaration of your worth handy and remember that it applies to you!

Self-worth should not be based on some other person's actions or opinions. True self-worth comes only through a solid relationship with Heavenly Father and the Savior and through experiencing Their love. By developing that connection, we will come to understand that our worth is immeasurable. Our self-worth (and relationship with God) must originate primarily from inside our souls. We cannot weather well the fiery trials imposed by a spouse's addiction or unfaithfulness unless there is a strong sense of self from a powerful bond with our Heavenly Father.

Moroni said that "despair cometh because of iniquity" (Moroni 10:22). Our despair may be the natural consequence of our own sins, or it may result from the sins of those we love. The sexual betrayal of a spouse initiates a brutal crushing of our self-image. It is the ultimate form of rejection and disrespect. If we have allowed our feelings of self-worth to depend upon the opinions of our spouse, it will surely result in despair. But if we have a close and strong relationship with the Lord, we will know that we are of worth regardless of what our spouse says or does.

YOUR RESPONSIBILITY

Therefore, you have some great responsibilities to yourself and to your marriage. Obviously, it is imperative that you turn to your Heavenly Father in faith. Feast upon His word. Look for personal answers in the scriptures. Search out His will for you. These things do not come without effort and time given daily. Pray often. Listen to the still, small voice. Keep a journal. In these ways a relationship with God will grow and flourish and you will be strengthened to bear your trials with honor.

Maintain your integrity. Act only according to what you know is right and what you instinctively feel is right. Some women have told me that their husbands convinced them to participate in pornographic exposure or unnatural sexual activities along with them. Thinking they were helping their marital relationship, these women discovered, as I did, that it only undermined their relationship with the Lord and drove them into further despair. They suffered a loss of self and were left with a feeling of being used. Those types of "concessions" have absolutely nothing to do with love, with building a good marriage, or with any of a dozen other excuses a spouse may have given in an effort to get his wife to help satisfy his lust-filled hungers. Be true to yourself. Maintain your own integrity.

BLAME

Typical of many letters we've received, one distressed wife wrote: "I spent many years turning myself inside out to be a better person because he told me— and I believed him—that the problems were my fault. So I reached and stretched and grieved while he sat on the truth and watched me self-destruct." She went on, "Now he accuses me of holding us up; of being unforgiving. It is my fault. Of course, he is still slipping into porn, but now he says I am driving him to it with my unforgiving attitude."

In a wonderful article entitled, "Repentance,"[2] F. Burton Howard wrote: "The habit of shifting the burden of guilt onto someone else, while perhaps understandable... has an ancient but not honorable tradition. Cain blamed God when his sacrifice was not accepted . . . (Moses 5:38). Laman and Lemuel blamed Nephi for nearly all their troubles (See 1 Ne. 16:35–38). Pilate blamed the Jews when he condoned the crucifixion of the Savior, in whom he found 'no fault' (Luke 23:4; see also Matt. 27:24). Elder Howard's point was, "Unwillingness to accept the responsibility for and consequences of one's actions is an all-too-common condition in today's world. When faced with the consequences of transgression, rather than looking to ourselves as the source of the discomfort which always accompanies sin, many of us tend to blame someone else." Every person is liable for his own sins and must, therefore, take the initiative to repent and to change.

Likewise, accepting blame for another's problems is wrong. It is also hurtful to him because, in doing so, you step between him and his Savior, who is the only One who can help him make the changes he needs to make in himself. It is important to understand that only Jesus Christ was authorized to take upon himself the sins of others.

2 See *Ensign*, May 1991, pp. 12-13.

Be advised that it does not matter if you weigh four hundred pounds, have zits or are cold in bed, you still are not in any way responsible for your husband's sin, his repentance, or his rescue. Every person on this earth, who is accountable, is responsible for his or her own salvation. It is between you and Jesus Christ for your salvation, and it is between your spouse and Jesus Christ for his.

YOUR CHILDREN

After discovering her husband's fascination with pornography and knowing of his habit of masturbation, one woman wrote: "I am very confused. I do not know where to turn. I think about it constantly. I want to scream at my husband for putting me into this situation . . . I worry about my children and wonder if they are safe. I have a teen-aged daughter and a young son. I wonder if I should kick him out of the house and tell him to choose pornography or his family. The problem is, I love him. He has good qualities. He is the father of my children . . . I guess my question is—is this something I need to worry about or am I making it bigger than it is?"

I will explain why it is impossible to make it bigger than it is! When our bishop came to our home to see us the morning after Gerald's confession to me, I asked him, "What should I do? Should I make him leave our home or initiate a divorce?" Not feeling it was his place to actually tell me what to do in this circumstance, he nevertheless gave inspired counsel that became the measuring rod of our relationship during the trying times to come.

"Sister Curtis," he carefully said, "Only you can make that decision. But I would suggest that you look to your children and decide whether or not their father's presence in the home is detrimental to them. If it is, then he should leave. If not, perhaps it would be better for him to stay." That became my standard and I told my husband about it. One time my resolve was tested. One of our little children discovered some pornographic magazines Gerald had hidden in our home and questioningly reported it to me. I was furious! It was bad enough that he was subject to its awful, evil influence, but one of my children now was contaminated and I would not stand for that. I told him this was his only chance to remain with our family; that if it ever happened again, he would have to leave. At the time, I was horrified to think that may have to actually happen, and I had no idea how we would survive if he left. But I was strong enough to carry it out because I knew the counsel I had been given was from the Lord. Gerald knew I was iron-willed about it and, thankfully, never again brought anything of that nature into our home.

I am confident of these two things: First, the Holy Spirit will not dwell in an unclean or immoral environment. Pornography in any of its many forms is ugly, evil and soul-destroying. If anyone, while in the home, even privately, views pornography, lusts and/or abuses himself, it brings a spirit into the home that you do not want. The devils rejoice to find such a place to dwell. That so-called "private" practice will drive the Holy Spirit out of a home and prohibit the receiving of promptings that are needed to wage a victorious battle against the power of the adversary.

Secondly, it is our responsibility as mothers to care for and protect our children; to do all in our power to bring them up safely and in the nurture and admonition of the Lord; and to teach them to pray and to feel the Holy Ghost in their lives. I believe the Lord will require an accounting at our hands of these things. It is a duty to be taken seriously—even to the necessity of ejecting from our home all that would infringe upon this responsibility. I think the Lord expects that of mothers—to pray and to be in tune with the Spirit so that their children may be protected from physical and spiritual harm.

Based upon these two premises, it is imperative that we "draw a line." Today, a parent's responsibility to train and protect their children from disease, accident and harm is broadened to an almost impossible task. The only protection to be found is in homes where there is strict observance of Christian principles and meticulous, attentive care in the avoidance of opportunity to indulge curiosity or wicked fantasy. Children must be protected from this pornographic plague, armed against the loss of their spiritual identity and strengthened to survive the undulating standards of ethics and morality that challenge even the elect among families in the Church.

There is a big difference in being a support to your husband and in being an "enabler" of his sinful habits and choices. The line between them is a fine line and can only be drawn successfully by putting faith in the Lord and scrupulously following His promptings. You must allow your husband his agency, extend love and compassion, be humble and yet, have the courage of your convictions and learn to be firm when righteous principles are abrogated.

SELF-RIGHTEOUSNESS

I must insert a caution at this point. The necessity of "taking a stand," or of "drawing a line" can bring with it the temptation to be sanctimonious, holier-than-thou, or self-righteous. Satan will do all he can to derail your attempts at preserving your family. His favorite tactic among wives of porn addicts seems to be to encourage either weak-willed passivity or strong-willed self-righteousness. Neither is acceptable to the Lord and neither will result in a victory for the family.

The quality of submissiveness is good, but only if it is submission to the will of God and to righteous priesthood leaders. We must always recognize our own limitations and faults and seek to overcome them. It is vital that we as women focus on our own need for improvement more than we dwell upon our spouse's need for change. If we will be meek in our relationship with God, He will teach us what we must learn and help us to master the lessons He has designed to bring us closer to Him. Humility should be the paramount quality we evidence in our supplications to our Heavenly Father. But we must draw strength from Him to do all that He commands us and will require of us. With His help we must be able to "stand for something," as President Hinckley advises, and to be strong and courageous in the battle against sin.

A great resource that will keep us humble, yet enable us to be firm, is our priesthood leadership and priesthood blessings. Yet, so many women hesitate to talk to their bishops because they feel, in some way, they might be betraying their husbands. This stems from a false sense of nobility and is wrong. These are blessings we need and deserve as we raise our children and try to stand firm in righteousness.

Some years after Gerald's rebaptism, I felt a particular need of a bishop's blessing to help me regain my perspective and give me strength to withstand the cutting and critical jabs being flung at me by my depressive husband. I knew I would be telling the bishop things that would disparage Gerald, but I needed the strength I would get from his counsel and a priesthood blessing. I told Gerald what I was going to do and asked if he'd like to accompany me. He was stung, but understood that I had every right to seek the blessing I desired. I wasn't going there to "tattle" on him, but rather to gain a blessing for myself and to work out my own weaknesses. We as women have not only the right, but the duty to use every available resource in fulfilling our responsibilities to ourselves, our husbands and our children.

BE A LIGHT, NOT A JUDGE

When it comes right down to it, none of us are finished products. We are all still struggling to live the best we can, to learn to make correct choices, and to gain the power to return to God who will finish us. No one likes to be judged and found wanting by anyone but God. He is the only One who can help fill in the gaps and polish the rough edges of our characters. Meanwhile, we must accept the means He uses to accomplish that objective. I have come to appreciate that our marriage problems were His tools in my development. He used them for Gerald as well.

Improving the marriage never starts with changing your spouse. It always begins with changing yourself. If we wives and mothers had our way, I fear we would all want to decide for ourselves what qualities our husbands and children were lacking, make the decisions for them to change, engineer their choices and their repentance, and . . . voila! . . . poof! . . . they would be magically transformed into knights in shining armor who would conquer the world and lovingly pamper and protect us into a bright future. (So much for free agency!) However, what is required is that we cease to focus on our loved ones' failures, patiently wait upon the Lord's timetable, and look to our own improvement.

P.S. WHAT ABOUT DIVORCE?

Almost the first question that I faced after I learned of Gerald's unfaithfulness was whether or not we should divorce. That question would arise again and again through the years as we confronted each new challenge to our marriage covenants, and it is a question that many couples face when they learn of a spouse's infidelity.

As I explained in Chapter Six, I had always believed that, in the case of infidelity, divorce was an option to be seriously considered and probably sought. However, when Gerald confessed his adultery, I was unsure of that assumption and needed to know the Lord's will.

I think that even the most enlightened of priesthood leaders may have encouraged me to seek a divorce had they foreseen the grief the next eighteen years of struggle would bring to our family. Yet our Heavenly Father, while seeing my present and coming sorrow, knew that what lay ahead for Gerald and me was an eternity of joy and love as soon as we could prepare ourselves to receive it. Thus, with my bishop's counsel, I was inspired to reject divorce as a solution and to begin the long struggle that would take half a lifetime to resolve.

MARRIAGE—A CONTRACT

It is my opinion that the true meaning of commitment has been lost in today's world. Fettered by traditions of divorce, we make promises of love and fidelity that are easily broken and cast aside at the slightest provocation.

Marriage never was easy. It may never be. It brings with it sacrifice, sharing, and a demand for great selflessness. . . . It has come to be a common thing to talk about divorce. The minute there is a little crisis or a little argument in the family, we talk about divorce, and we rush to see an attorney. This is not the way of the Lord. We should go back and adjust our problems and make our marriage compatible and sweet and blessed [Spencer W. Kimball, *Marriage and Divorce*, pp. 12, 30–31].

To illustrate societal impact on the level of our commitment to each other and to our contracts, one need only remember stories of a bygone day when "a man's word was his bond." Contracts were made with only a shake of the hands, and then scrupulously kept. The Book of Mormon also provides examples of such traditions of trust. For example, Nephi tells us how Laban's servant, Zoram, gave an oath that he would not try to escape or to warn the Jews concerning their flight into the wilderness with the brass plates. Because, in those times, one could count on people to keep their promises, Nephi said, "And it came to pass that when Zoram had made an oath unto us, our fears did cease concerning him" (1 Nephi 4:37).

> In an eternal marriage, the thought of ending what began with a covenant between God and each other simply has little place. When challenges come and our individual weaknesses are revealed, the remedy is to repent, improve, and apologize, not to separate or divorce. When we make covenants with the Lord and our eternal companion, we should do everything in our power to honor the terms [Marlin K. Jensen, *Ensign*, Oct. 1994, p.51].

How regrettable it is that such traditions of trust are so rare in our world today. Breaking contracts and covenants is hardly considered wrongdoing. Sadly, many people believe they need only feel some little suffering or heartache before the first thought that comes to mind is one of escaping the obligations that incur the heartache—such as marriage difficulties. President Gordon B. Hinckley has stated:

> There may be now and again a legitimate cause for divorce. I am not one to say that it is never justified. But I say without hesitation that this plague among us, which seems to be growing everywhere, is not of God, but rather is the work of the adversary of righteousness and peace and truth. You need not be its victims [*Ensign*, May 1991, 74, as quoted in "Mending Our Marriage," *Ensign*, Oct. 1996, p.51].

The consideration we give to the constant suggestions of our adversary is in large part dependant upon the tradition of our own family history. If divorce has been the perceived solution to the marital troubles of our parents or grandparents, it is easily deemed appropriate as a solution to our own troubles. During Gerald's "depression years" when our marriage relationship particularly deteriorated into despair and hopelessness, Gerald's frequently suggested way out of our problems was divorce. That was the example or "tradition" he had inherited from his family. Only the "tradition" of my parents and grandparents, who had weathered life's difficult storms without separation or divorce, allowed me to continually refute that suggestion as a solution to our problems. Because of my family "tradition," I remained convinced another solution could be found. And because of my stubbornness, our marriage survived to a day when it could be healed by the grace of God and His great goodness toward us.

"CAST THY BURDEN UPON THE LORD[3]"

Our marriage improved a great deal after the Lord rescued Gerald from his addiction to pornography. It continued to improve following his rebaptism. But when he was attacked by the depression years, our marriage became almost intolerable. As we struggled through those up-and-down cycles of depression, I finally realized it may never get any better and once again, I had to decide whether I should stay with him or not. He seemed to constantly suggest divorce, but I was still loath to consider it as a justifiable option. Our troubles did not presently threaten the well-being of the children as most of them had left to make lives of their own. And I continued to hope that, with the Lord's help, Gerald's seeming hatred and dissatisfaction with me would someday be replaced by consideration and love.

As I read in The Book of Mormon *the account of how the Lord eased the unjust suffering of Alma's people during their captivity, I found consolation, knowing he could ease my marriage burdens in the same manner.*

> And I will also ease the burdens which are put upon your shoulders, that even you cannot feel them upon your backs, even while you are in bondage; and this will I do that ye may stand as witnesses for me hereafter, and that ye may know of a surety that I, the Lord God, do visit my people in their afflictions.

> And now it came to pass that the burdens which were laid upon Alma and his brethren were made light; yea, the Lord did strengthen them that they could bear up their burdens with ease, and they did submit cheerfully and with patience to all the will of the Lord [Mosiah 24:14-15].

So often we pray to have our burdens removed, but in the Lord's wisdom, He answers that we must bear them for a time so that a greater blessing might be received. In retrospect, with the happiness we now have in our union, I can understand that those first thirty-five years of our marriage were suffered so that we could learn the lessons we each needed to enable us to receive an eternity of joy. But I never could have endured those hard years without God's grace, which lightened my burdens and enabled me to bear them, as He did for Alma and his people.

---

3 Psalms 55:22

Some couples may become discouraged at times and want to terminate the relationship. Although there may be instances where divorce is the only answer, there also exists the danger of uprooting something with potential good—just to get rid of something else that temporarily appears to be bad [Brent A. Barlow, *Ensign*, Oct. 1983, p.44].

Nevertheless, in our human condition, sadly, divorce is sometimes a necessary option. Hence, we must be careful to seek the will and guidance of the Lord.

REVELATION—A NECESSITY

While this mortal life is meant to be fraught with struggle, heartache and suffering as we all learn life's lessons and turn to God for strength, there is some suffering that our Heavenly Father does not expect us to indefinitely endure. As stated in the Ensign magazine, "Not all decisions to divorce, however, are made selfishly or impulsively. There are cases in which continuing a marriage relationship may result in spiritual, and possibly physical, destruction for a spouse and the children. But it should always be remembered that through forgiveness and repentance, even destructive relationships can improve if a selfish, abusive, or unfaithful spouse has the desire and shows the commitment to change" (S. Brent Scharman, "For Better, for Worse, for Always," Ensign, June 1991, p.27).

So how can we know whether we should stand by an unrepentant spouse, or ask him to leave? Simply by revelation! Only the Lord can foresee our future. Only He knows the covenants and contracts we entered into in our premortal state and which may be part of the reason for our present trials. Only God knows which strengths we need and which struggles will provide them for us as we seek to return to Him and enjoy an eternity of happiness.

Individuals contemplating divorce for even the most valid of reasons will be able to make wise decisions only after sincere prayer and careful weighing of the alternatives—seeking the guidance of the Holy Ghost as decisions are made [S. Brent Scharman, "For Better, for Worse, for Always," *Ensign*, June 1991, p.27].

I am a witness, along with the author of "Mending our Marriage" in the October 1996 Ensign, that " . . . for some couples it may take years to overcome causes of marital unhappiness while for others the challenges may tax the limits of their ability to endure and lead to divorce. The efforts to do one's best and apply gospel principles are both required and worth the necessary sacrifices. Indeed, obedience to the principles of righteous living has its own rewards (see D&C 58:2-4), such as spiritual strength and freedom from regret. Thus fortified for having drawn closer to the Lord, he will guide us aright in our trials (see D&C 88:63-64)."

IT IS WORTH IT!

Those who read Gerald's first book, The Worth of A Soul, *may have assumed that, though we went through hell for a time, everything was taken care of and magically fixed by the end of the book. When it was written, that was what we believed. However, we have come to realize that when sin is indulged and covenants are broken, it takes more than a wave of a spiritual wand to fix the damage. Trust has been lost. Relationships have unraveled. Unity is undone and stability is nonexistent. Though there is hope and reason to continue on, time is needed to validate renewed promises and to rebuild trust.*

One woman said:

"Although I considered my husband's problems to be the source of my greatest trials, I found they also served in the end to bring both of us along separate and personal pathways to Jesus Christ" ["Mending Our Marriage," *Ensign,* Oct. 1996, p 47].

The value of a practical relationship with Jesus Christ is priceless. The added value of knowing yourself and of seeing yourself as God sees you is also incalculable. The price you pay to learn humility, meekness, faithfulness and spiritual strength to a much greater degree than ever before is high, but well worth it! An unshakeable testimony of the actuality of God and of His love is also worth whatever price we must pay.

The comparatively small sacrifice the Lord required of Gerald and I to go on a mission resulted in the resurrection of our love for each other, the restoration of unity into our marriage and a joy of companionship that far outweighs whatever relatively puny offering we may have given while serving our mission together. In this case, the Lord's timetable was far better than my own. We did not have to wait for "the next life" to receive the miracle of restoration. For the first time, untainted by the world, we experience love in being together. Both of us have come to know ourselves, to recognize the Spirit and to feel joy in our companionship. Is that worth what we have suffered and sacrificed and learned? Unqualifiedly, YES!

Ye cannot behold with your natural eyes, for the present time, the design of your God concerning those things which shall come hereafter, and the glory which shall follow after much tribulation [D&C 58:3].

In summary, my life's experience and the letters I have received from others teach me that casualties and victims of societal ills abound all around us and among us. There is almost no home that is unaffected in some way. The need becomes ever more imperative to call upon the Lord, to come unto Christ, to draw near to God as we sojourn through this world of sin and attempt to usher our families into the celestial kingdom unscathed and untarnished. We simply cannot do it alone. Now, more than ever before, we absolutely must hearken to the counsel of our leaders and partner with God in our individual and parental responsibilities. We must learn to hear and hearken to the voice of the Spirit. Anything less is doomed to fall victim to Satan and to the ills and plagues with which he has infected our world.

As one sister to another, I testify that guidance, peace and comfort is available through Jesus Christ. Heavenly Father will put His arms of love around you and bestow upon you every good blessing. The price we pay for that is a willingness to sacrifice and to do all God requires of us in the time and in the manner that He requires it.

LoAnne

DISCIPLINARY COUNCILS

This mortal life is a school which furnishes important courses of instruction as we prepare for eternity by learning to control our thoughts and desires and to apply gospel principles in our daily living. But unlike public schools, where the same basic curriculums are required for graduation, the Lord customizes our course work to our individual needs. While there are many fundamental principles we must all learn and obey, no one will "graduate" to eternal life unless they master the "homework" the Lord designs for their individual progress and perfection.

> For if you will that I give unto you a place in the celestial world, you must prepare yourselves by doing the things which I have commanded you and required of you [D&C 78:7].

If we wish to rise above the natural man and attain fulfillment of the Savior's promises, we need to stop resenting our spiritual "homework" and start trusting the Lord, who is carefully choosing the lessons we need most. Brigham Young said, "Every trial and experience you have passed through is necessary for your salvation" (Discourses of Brigham Young, Salt Lake City: Deseret Book Co., 1954, p. 345, as quoted in the 1976 *Priesthood Manual*, p. 228, or *Ensign*, July 1986, p. 31). Resenting the lessons, which are "necessary" for our salvation, is like paying tuition to go to college and then resenting the homework.

Serious transgression may limit God's ability to be with us and bless us, but it does not prevent Him from loving us. Excommunication is separation from the *organized church*, not from *God*, "for he hath said, I will never leave thee, nor forsake thee" (Hebrews 13:5). And yet He has warned that He will not be mocked. (See 2 Nephi 26:11; D&C 1:33; 63:58.) Just as God cannot save us in spite of our disobedience, so He cannot force His love upon us if we refuse to accept it. Consequently, when we choose to openly and wickedly flout His commandments, He may temporarily withhold His Spirit from us in the hope that experiencing the pain and loneliness of living without Him will motivate us to repent. "If you keep not my commandments," the Savior warned, "the love of the Father shall not continue with you, therefore you shall walk in darkness" (D&C 95:12). Notice, this verse does not say that God would stop loving us because we made wrong choices. That never happens. Rather, we will not be able to feel or to receive His love when we willfully walk in darkness.

> Who [or what] shall separate us from the love of Christ? Shall tribulation, or distress, or persecution, or famine, or nakedness, or peril, or sword [or excommunication]?
>
> Nay, in all these things we are more than conquerors, through him that loved us. For I am persuaded, that neither death, nor life . . . nor height, nor depth [of sin], nor any other [circumstance] shall be able to separate us from the love of God, which is in Christ Jesus our Lord [Romans 8:35, 37-39].

King Benjamin explained that it is really *we*, rather than *God*, who do the withdrawing: "And now, I say unto you, my brethren, that after ye have known and have taught all these things, if ye should transgress and go contrary to that which has been spoken, that *ye do withdraw yourselves* from the Spirit of the Lord, that it may have no place in you to guide you in wisdom's paths that ye may be blessed, prospered, and preserved" (Mosiah 2:36). His love is still there, and behind the scenes, He is waiting and hoping that we learn the needed lessons and return to Him quickly. "For a small moment have I forsaken thee; but with great mercies will I gather thee. In a little wrath I hid my face from thee for a moment; but with everlasting kindness will I have mercy on thee, saith the Lord thy Redeemer" (Isaiah 54:7-8). Although I did not understand this when I encountered my own disciplinary council, I now know that excommunication was the kindest and most loving thing Heavenly Father could have done for me, considering the restrictive circumstances my disobedience had forced upon Him.

Over the years I have met many excommunicants who have the same conviction. One of them was a man who was scorned by his family. He lost his children as well as his marriage. He also lost his business. One might expect such a person to feel anger and bitterness against the Church and all those who had judged and rejected him. Yet this man was happy and hopeful as he patiently relearned the gospel and made his way back. He seemed surprised when I asked him why he wasn't bitter about the discipline and all that it had cost him. As he expressed gratitude for the increased spirituality he was gaining through his experience, he likened his excommunication to a stop sign. He told me that as he had ignored the commandments and his covenants, it was as if he had been speeding down the road of sin, heading straight for hell. But the Lord and the Church had loved him enough to put a stop sign right in his path. That abrupt judgment gave him the opportunity to make eternal choices: the choice to continue downward, if he so wished, or to turn around and repent. He said, "What good would it do for me to waste my life standing there kicking at the stop sign?" I remember his example anytime I hear someone criticize the Lord's divinely revealed plan of church discipline.

Elder Robert L. Simpson told a similar story:

> The brief episode I am about to relate is true, and the facts are accurate. Those who were present will never forget them. The hour was very late and the room was quiet except for the audible sobs of a young man who had just received the verdict of a Church court. Justice had taken its true course. There had been no alternative. The unanimous decision, following serious deliberation, fasting, and prayer, was for excommunication.

> After several minutes, his face reflecting his weariness, the young man looked up and his voice broke the silence. "I have just lost the most precious thing in my life," he said, "and nothing will stand in my way until I have regained it." The process leading up to the court had not been an easy one. It had taken great courage, a most important factor for every person who has seriously slipped but wants to get back on the Lord's side.

> This man had just taken his first giant step back. As an excommunicated member of the Church, determined in his heart to make things right, he was far better off than he had been just a few days before with his membership intact, but with deceit in his heart that seemed to shout the word hypocrite with every move he made toward doing something in the Church.

> This episode took place a few years ago. The young man's pledge has been fulfilled, and in my opinion, no member of the Church stands on firmer ground than the man who has had the courage to unburden himself to his priesthood authority and to set things in order with his Maker. What a relief it must be for him to have once again the peace of mind that "passeth all understanding" ["Courts of Love," *Ensign*, July 1972, pp. 48-49].

COURTS OF LOVE

While being called into a church disciplinary council and there receiving a judgment of disfellowshipment or excommunication can certainly *seem* like vindictive punishment, it is not. I am convinced that church discipline is not something that happens **to** you—it happens **for** you.

> Priesthood courts of the Church are not courts of retribution. They are courts of love. Oh, that members of the Church could understand this one fact. The adversary places a fear in the heart that makes it difficult for the transgressor to do what needs to be done; and in the words of James E. Talmage, "As the time of repentance is procrastinated, the ability to repent grows weaker; neglect of opportunity in holy things develops inability" (*Church News*, March 25, 1972). This simply means that doing what needs to be done will never be easier than now. As in all other paths and guideposts that have been provided for us to achieve our eternal destiny of exaltation, there are no shortcuts [Robert L. Simpson, "Courts of Love," *Ensign*, July 1972, p. 49].

When a person's leg is hopelessly infected with gangrene and amputation is required, the surgery should not be viewed as a negative procedure, but a positive one. It is the only remedy that would enable the individual to have a healthy life. And so it is with the spiritual life of the excommunicant. If the spiritual fault in his or her life was so minor that it only required a Band-aid level of treatment, the Lord would not require the major surgery of excommunication. When such a procedure is required, it must also be viewed as a positive step toward spiritual health. Unlike an amputation, however, excommunication need not be permanent. Its effects can be reversed and totally eradicated from one's life and can become a valuable experience.

> My son, despise not the chastening of the Lord; neither be weary of his correction: For whom the Lord loveth, he correcteth; even as a father the son in whom he delighteth [Proverbs 3:11-12].

Unfortunately, some priesthood leaders avoid established Church discipline procedures by mistaking leniency for mercy. While their intent may be kind, denying someone who needs the privilege of starting over, which is provided by Church discipline, is neither kind, helpful nor merciful. I learned the truth of this principle while in attendance at a priesthood support group for excommunicants who were helping each other in the repentance process. The guest speaker was a former stake president. He made the remark that in all his years of service, he had never once excommunicated "a sincerely repentant person." It was as if he was saying that every person who *has been* excommunicated is neither sincere nor repentant.

In response to his statement, an attractive young woman began to weep. Through her tears, she told us that she had committed fornication many years before and how empty she had felt when her bishop brushed her confession aside with no real concern or action. She did the best she could to repent, but eventually, now living in a different ward, it had happened again. The second bishop chastised her rather sternly, but took no disciplinary action. Again she struggled to repent, but felt completely alone in the effort. Finally, once again in a new ward, it happened a third time. She looked that former stake president in the eye as she expressed her deep gratitude that at last she had a bishop who cared enough about her to hold a disciplinary council; to excommunicate her and give her an opportunity to finally get things right with the Lord. She expressed her conviction that if her first bishop had possessed the courage and the caring to hold a disciplinary council for her, she most likely would never have suffered the other two failures.

President Spencer W. Kimball emphasized that conducting a Church council to hold someone accountable for serious transgression is not just a Church policy, but is a commandment from God. "It is so easy to let our sympathies carry us out of proportion; and when a man has committed sin, he must suffer. It is an absolute requirement—not by the bishop—but it is a requirement by nature and by the very part of a man" (*Ensign*, May 1975, p. 78).

> We believe that all religious societies have a right to deal with their members for disorderly conduct, according to the rules and regulations of such societies; provided that such dealings be for fellowship and good standing; but we do not believe that any religious society has authority to try men on the fight of property or life, to take from them this world's goods, or to put them in jeopardy of either life or limb, or to inflict any physical punishment upon them. They can only excommunicate them from their society, and withdraw from them their fellowship [D&C 134:10].

Such action is taken in the hope of reclaiming the person who has jeopardized their salvation by disobedience and also to preserve the purity and integrity of Church standards. "And this ye shall do that God may be glorified—not because ye forgive not, having not compassion, but that ye may be justified in the eyes of the law, that ye may not offend him who is your lawgiver" (D&C 64:13). If the Church were to allow major corruption in the membership to go unchallenged, it would not only diminish the sanctity of what we stand for, but also the availability of the Spirit to Church leaders, whose inaction would have offended God. As George Q. Cannon, of the First Presidency, said:

> The Spirit of God would undoubtedly be so grieved that it would forsake not only those who are guilty of these acts, but it would withdraw itself from those who would suffer them to be done in our midst unchecked and unrebuked; and from the President of the Church down, throughout the entire ranks of the priesthood, there would be a loss of the Spirit of God, a withdrawal of His gifts and blessing and His power, because of their not taking the proper measures to check and to expose their iniquity [*Journal of Discourses*, 26:139, as quoted by Spencer W. Kimball in the *Ensign*, May 1975, p. 78].

Since the Lord has repeatedly emphasized that He cannot ignore or turn aside from our sins, neither should Church leaders. Consider the warning President Kimball gave to priesthood leaders: "We are concerned that too many times the interviewing leader in his personal sympathies for the transgressor, and in his love perhaps for the family of the transgressor, is inclined to waive the discipline which that transgressor demands. Too often a transgressor is forgiven and all penalties waived when that person should have been disfellowshipped or excommunicated. Too often a sinner is disfellowshipped when he or she should have been excommunicated (Spencer W. Kimball, "To Bear the Priesthood Worthily," *Ensign*, May 1975, p. 78). He then quoted President John Taylor's warning to passive priesthood leaders who mistake taking no action for mercy:

> I have heard of some bishops who have been seeking to cover up the iniquities of men; I tell them, in the name of God, they will have to bear them themselves, and meet that judgment; and I tell you that any man who tampers with iniquity, he will have to bear that iniquity, and if any of you want to partake of the sins of men, or uphold them, you will have to bear them. Do you hear it, you bishops and you presidents? God will require it at your hands. You are not placed in position to tamper with principles of

righteousness, nor to cover up the infamies and corruptions of men [Conference Report, April 1880, p. 78, as quoted in *Ensign*, May 1975, p. 78].

Failing to hold a person accountable for their mistakes encourages the continuation of those mistakes. Mercy without justice and accountability is neither loving nor kind.

TOTAL FORGIVENESS

One of the lessons I have learned through my excommunication experience is that the most important thing to the Lord, once we have repented, is not the mistakes we have made, but rather, what we learned from them and how we choose to live as a result. When Christ makes us new, our past mistakes are no longer important. There is no condemnation for mistakes or choices that we have abandoned. Remember! No matter how filthy or wicked our past may have been, our future is spotless! Elder Theodore M. Burton, of the First Quorum of the Seventy, whose assignment it was to assist excommunicants in returning to the Church, once said of his duties:

> I have been asked the question, "Isn't it depressing to have to review the sins and transgressions of people involved in such difficulties?" It would be if I were looking for sins and transgressions. But I am working with people who are repenting. These are sons and daughters of God who have made mistakes—some of them very serious. But *they are not sinners.* They *were* sinners in the past but have learned through bitter experience the heartbreak that results from disobedience to God's laws. Now they are no longer sinners. They are God's repentant children who want to come back to Him and are striving to do so ["Let Mercy Temper Justice," *Ensign*, Nov. 1985, p. 64].

Unfortunately, many former excommunicants cannot forgive themselves and let go of the past—even after they are rebaptized. When excommunication is over, it should be *over!* It is not pleasing to a forgiving Heavenly Father when His children reject the blessings of the Atonement and insist on dragging past sins into their future. It is Satan's strategy to make us feel guilty for having weaknesses, or for needing repentance and forgiveness. For example, the scriptures emphasize, "Blessed is he whose transgression is forgiven, whose sin is covered" (Romans 4:7; see also Psalms 32:1). But nowhere do the scriptures say, or even *hint* at the idea: "Blessed are they who never *need* forgiveness," because there is no such person.

Similarly, the Lord also emphasized, "Blessed are they who will repent and turn unto me" (Helaman 13:11). And, "Blessed are they who will repent and hearken unto the voice of the Lord their God; for these are they that shall be saved" (Helaman 12:23). Thus the Lord said, "And because thou has seen thy weakness thou shalt be made strong, even unto the sitting down in the place which I have prepared in the mansions of my Father" (Ether 12:37).

I do not believe that God keeps score of repented sins! (See Psalms 79:8; 130:3-4.) "I, even I, am he that blotteth out thy transgressions for mine own sake, and will not remember thy sins" (Isaiah 43:25).[1] So total is the dismissal of our past resolved sins from Christ's memory that when we come before Him in judgment, those forgiven sins "that he hath committed, they shall not [even] be mentioned unto him" (Ezekiel 18:22). As Elder Simpson emphasized:

> What a glorious plan this is! How reassuring to know that we all have hope for a total blessing, in spite of all the mistakes we have made; that there might be complete fulfillment; that we might enter his holy presence with our family units.
>
> Even excommunication from this church is not the end of the world; and if this process is necessary in carrying out true justice, I bear you my personal and solemn witness that even this extreme penalty of excommunication can be the first giant step back, provided there follows a sincere submission to the Spirit and faith in the authenticity of God's plan [Robert L. Simpson, "Courts of Love," *Ensign*, July 1972, p. 49].

---

1 For similar reference about the Lord dismissing such things "for his own sake," see Psalms 23:3; 25:11; 31:3; Isaiah 48:9; Ephesians 4:32; D&C 64:3.

UNDERSTANDING GRACE

One of the most baffling parts of my excommunication experience was the puzzle of how LoAnne could endure the insufferable way that I treated her and the children during those two horrible years of buffeting, when my emotions were under satanic influence. I totally deserved to be rejected. No one would have criticized or condemned her for insisting that I leave the home, not just because my presence was so evil and depressing, but because there was not the slightest clue that I would ever improve.

Yet she bore the multitude of injustices that I imposed upon her and the children patiently and kindly, almost passively. Her response to my cruel abuse was like the silent, submissive attitude of the Savior as He allowed the Jews and Romans to heap indignity after indignity upon Him. I don't think there are very many women who would have willingly endured what she did.

How could my wife endure that suffering without growing bitter, protesting, retaliating or fighting back? As she explained in chapter ten, the truth is that, *on her own*, she could not have reacted to me in that truly Christ-like manner. No one could, and the wonderful message of God's love and grace is that He doesn't expect us to. Not without His divine assistance. Surely this knowledge should give great encouragement to all who are suffering through similar difficulties.

When Alma's recent converts were found and placed in bondage by their Lamanite enemies, the Lord gave them this promise of grace: "I will . . . ease the burdens which are put upon your shoulders, that even you cannot feel them upon your backs, even while you are in bondage . . . that ye may know of a surety that I, the Lord God, do visit my people in their afflictions" (Mosiah 24:14).

While the Lord may not immediately remove or free us from our painful circumstances, He is always ready and eager to strengthen and assist every person who is submissively and obediently facing over-whelming challenges that go beyond their ability to handle. That is what grace is. That is what it does. As the Bible Dictionary states:

> The main idea of the word [grace] is a divine means of help or strength, given through the bounteous mercy and love of Jesus Christ. It is likewise through the grace of the Lord that individu-als, through faith in the Atonement of Jesus Christ and repentance of their sins, receive strength and assistance to do good works that they otherwise would not be able to maintain if left to their own means. This grace is an enabling power that allows men and women to lay hold on eternal life and exaltation after they have expended their own best efforts [See Grace, p. 697].

Obeying every commandment and following Christ's example until we become like Him would be an incredibly unreachable goal for fallen mankind if we were left to achieve it by our abilities and merits alone. Thus, the necessity of grace. While the Lord expects us to use our own strengths and abilities to do as much for ourselves and others as we can, it will always be true that "it is by grace that we are saved after all we can do" (2 Nephi 25:23). Many people may lament over this verse, assuming that His grace could only bless us *sequentially*, after a lifetime of exhausting ourselves in doing "all" that could be humanly done. I do not believe it refers to the sequence of efforts and blessings at all. It is simply telling us the obvious truth that in spite of the very best efforts of the most righteous among us, it would still require His grace *in addition* to that effort, not after it.

Grace is not so much a *reward* to be received at the end of our struggles as it is a *partnership* that allows God to expand our own best efforts, as we progress through the lessons of mortality. It is imperative that we recognize that no one can ever do enough, by his own efforts, to live the obedient life that will result in exaltation. If we could, why would we need a Savior?

As the "natural man" (or woman) strives to overcome his personal weaknesses, faults, and the challenges of unwanted circumstances, it is normal to ignore this divine partnership and focus our confidence and reliance upon ourselves. After all, ever since we were children we've been waiting till we were grown up and could do it by ourselves. But the Savior has warned that unless we come to Him "as a little child," we will never become qualified to enter the kingdom of heaven. A child comes for *help*, not to prove his self-reliance.

There is a fine line that exists between our best efforts, that are both appropriate and necessary, and the well-intended but misleading "I-must-do-it-all-by-myself" attitude that can become self-defeating. The false belief that if we apply enough effort and determination, we can eventually become good enough for God, without His help in the becoming, is precisely the pride which kept me in captivity for so many years when Christ was both able and eager to free me. As the 1969-70 Gospel Doctrine manual stated:

> "I am the Way," the Savior tells those who hope to find the means, the way to create heaven. *Only in him can any man find the strength, the power and ability to live a godly life.* Only in Christ is there power to transform the human mind and the human heart . . . Only in Jesus Christ can any man learn the truth of what he is and how he can be changed from what he is to do the good for which he hopes [*In His Footsteps Today*, S.L.C., Utah: Deseret Sunday School Union, 1969, p. 4].

In a church that places emphasis on good works, self-sufficiency and enduring to the end, it is easy to feel guilty for needing help from God to be and to do what He has commanded us to do and to become. Indeed, I fear that "grace" is both a word and a subject that is sometimes scorned and dismissed as false Protestant doctrine. However, Latter-day Saint scriptures contain far more verses and revelations concerning this crucial doctrine than are in the Bible.

God never intended a competition between works and grace. His intent was a balance in the partnership. As Joseph Fielding Smith explained, "God . . . does not do for us one thing that we can do for ourselves, but requires of us that we do everything for ourselves that is within our power for our salvation. I think that is logical and reasonable. On the other hand, the Lord has done [or will do] everything for our salvation, that we could not do for ourselves . . . " (*Doctrines of Salvation*, 3 Vols. Compiled by Bruce R. McConkie, 6th Ed., S.L.C., Utah: Bookcraft, 1955, Vol. 2, p. 308).

One of the great messages of Christ feeding the multitudes with only a few loaves of bread and fishes is that no matter how insurmountable our challenges may appear, no matter how weak and inadequate we may be, we can always start right where we are, by using the limited resources and abilities that we *do* have, and then relying on His grace to expand our efforts to be sufficient to endure our hardships and accomplish our tasks. Because my wife's desire to be in harmony with the Lord's will was paramount in her heart, the Lord actually loaned her the ability to feel and act as He would want her to act! And this blessing is available to every person who is in need of similar help.[1]

The more that we mature spiritually, the more our *self*-centeredness and *self*-reliance must be surrendered to a *Christ*-centeredness and reliance upon *Him*. "We must do all that we can do. We must extend ourselves to the limit, we must stretch and bend the soul to its extremities. In the final analysis, however—at least when dealing with matters pertaining to spiritual growth and progression—it is not possible to 'pull ourselves up by our own bootstraps,' nor is it healthy to presume we can" (Robert L. Millet, *By Grace Are We Saved*, S.L.C., Utah: Bookcraft, 1989, p.100).

> Let us therefore come boldly unto the throne of grace, that we may obtain mercy, and find grace to help in time of need [Hebrews 4:16].

---

1 For additional explanations of how to receive this divine source of power, please see Chapters 1, 5, 12 and 13 in *Great Shall Be Your Joy*, which discuss His grace, sharing in His power and building a sure foundation on Christ that will lead us into *true* righteousness. See also Chater Four, "The Divine Parnership" in *Conquering Your Own Goliaths*.

"BORN AGAIN"

The General Authority who restored my temple and priesthood blessings also suggested, after our interview, that I write a book describing my conversion. It was his feeling that "Mormons" have a need to understand that everyone must be born again—even righteous, lifelong members who have not been guilty of any major transgression. It was his suggestion that led to the original version of *The Worth of a Soul* and that now compels me to share what I have learned about this doctrine.

After my spiritual transformation began, but before I was rebaptized and allowed to participate, I attended a priesthood class I shall never forget. The instructor, one of the most faithful high priests in our ward, began the class by announcing: "Our lesson today is about "being born again." And then he asked: "Don't you just *hate* that term?" I was shocked! *Hate* the very term and process that had saved my life? I wanted to stand and testify of what I had learned and experienced, but my lips were still sealed in public. I do not condemn his feeling, for I know there are many in the Church who identify the phrase "born again" as a Protestant term. I am certain he did not realize that this term occurs more frequently, and receives far greater textual dissertation, in Latter-day Saint scripture than in the Bible.

Scriptures that discuss the concepts of being "born again," and receiving "the mighty change" always present this process as a spiritual *necessity*—not as a suggestion. For example, Jesus said, "Except a man be born again, he cannot see the kingdom of God," and then counseled His confused audience, "Marvel not that I said unto thee, Ye *must* be born again" (John 3:3, 7). Alma emphasized the same theme: "I say unto you the aged, and also the middle aged, and the rising generation . . . that they must repent and be born again" for "the Spirit saith *if ye are not born again* ye cannot inherit the kingdom of heaven . . ." (Alma 5:49; 7:14).

Some of the people who marvel most over the need to be changed by God, instead of getting into heaven by their own good works, are righteous Church members who are sincerely trying to live the gospel and who do not feel guilty of any major sins. When Alma came out of his three days of being tutored by the Spirit, he testified: "And the Lord said unto me: Marvel not that *all mankind*, yea, men and women, *all* nations, kindreds, tongues and people [including members of the Church], must be born again: yea, born of God, *changed* from their carnal and fallen state, to a state of righteousness, being redeemed of God, becoming his sons and daughters" (Mosiah 27:25).

Such scriptures are referring to something far greater and more important than the mere physical act of baptism. Elder Bruce R. McConkie emphasized: "Mere compliance with the formality of the ordinance of baptism does not mean that a person has been born again" (*Mormon Doctrine*, Salt Lake City, Utah, Bookcraft Inc., second edition, 1966, p. 101). This is because, even after baptism, what is required is a *complete transformation* of the heart, desires, and fallen human nature. Preparing for the celestial kingdom is not based on controlling our evil desires with superhuman restraint and willpower, for then the evil is only caged and locked inside us like a ticking time bomb, just waiting for the right temptation to light the fuse. That is the natural man's way of trying to be good. It is the difference between relying on the mortal plan of merely *controlling* our bad habits, and allowing Christ to change our heart and give us a new birth so that we no longer *want* the sins. And nothing but the blood, Atonement, and grace of Jesus Christ can do that. Nonetheless, until we allow Jesus Christ to alter our hearts and desires, we will continue to suffer the constant struggle between the desires of the fallen flesh and the will of our spirit; between our fallen and natural-man will and God's will for us.

Paul emphasized the inner changes that must take place in full rebirth when he said: "If any man be in Christ, he [becomes] a *new creature*: old things are passed away; behold all things are become new"(2 Corinthians 5:17). Paul further emphasized the need to have our entire natures changed and transformed by the Spirit when he stressed our need to "*put off the old man* with his deeds," meaning setting aside the natural man ways of the flesh, and to "*put on the new man*, which after God is created in righteousness and true holiness" (Ephesians 4:24; see also Mosiah 27:25).

To receive the miracle of these divine transformations of mind, heart, personality and character, we must be totally dependent upon Christ. No matter how valiant and sincere we are, no matter how earnestly we try, *no one* can change their carnal nature by their own efforts, for "only Jesus Christ is uniquely qualified to provide that hope, that confidence, and that strength to overcome the world and rise above our human failings" (Ezra Taft Benson, *Ensign*, Nov. 1983, p. 6).

Every person on earth suffers from spiritual death (separation from God) to some degree. It is part of our mortal, fallen and "natural man" condition. Learning that we can never overcome this condition; i.e. restore spiritual life to ourselves, without the help of the Savior, may be one of the most difficult lessons we must learn. That was a major reason that my addictions lasted so long. Why hadn't He rescued me and healed me before when I tried so hard and begged so long? He couldn't help me while I was in the way, so busy trying to save myself that I had left no room for His help. While receiving His grace is not something we can earn, where much is given, much is required and God has a right to require the recipients to honor that gift by living a more Christlike life. He does not risk an investment of grace in people who will condemn themselves by trampling on it. And so, with all His infinite power and love, as much as He wanted to help me, the Lord would never override my agency. He waited until I realized with all of my being that I was never going to cure myself by myself, because only then could I open my heart to His power.

> *Only in Him* can any man find the strength, the power and the ability to live a godly life. Only in Christ is there power to transform the human mind and the human heart [Gospel Doctrine manual: *In His Footsteps Today*, Salt Lake City: Deseret Sunday School Union, 1969, p. 4].

During his last night in mortality, Jesus prophesied, "In this world ye shall have tribulation: but be of good cheer; I have overcome the world" (John 16:33). As we struggle to overcome our weaknesses and faults, why should the fact that our perfect Savior has overcome all the evils and weaknesses of mortality bring us "good cheer?" Simply because what He has done, He can enable us to do. The mortal part of us may cry, "But I have tried everything I know to overcome my faults—and still I fail." Think about this: Jesus Christ never fails. Therefore, we may be certain that if we continue to fail, it is because we are relying more upon our *own* power than upon *His*.

Perhaps we have earnestly tried to resist the evil within us, and yet have failed a thousand times. I have learned that as long as our past failures are the focus of our attention, we will continue to fail. As long as we continue to sow thoughts of fear, doubt, and lack of confidence in Christ because of *our* limited abilities to overcome, we will continue to reap a harvest of failure. On the other hand, when we focus our thoughts, faith, and attention on the fact that Jesus has already overcome every problem we could possibly face, then we can, through the miracle of His grace, be transformed and endowed with the all the knowledge and strength we need to overcome our difficulties and become like Him.

At this point, it is natural to protest, believing that you are not worthy or deserving of our Savior's help. Understand that the act of will which turns us toward Him in repentance entitles us to His help, *even before* we have the strength to keep our covenants flawlessly. His grace and redeeming power is a partnership with us *in* our struggles more than a reward at the *end* of the struggle. Cling to his promises, such as, "I will fight your battles" (D&C 105:14), "I will also save you from all your uncleanness" (Ezekiel 36:29), and "I am able to make you holy" (D&C 60:7). This, He is both *anxious* and *able* to do, if we will only allow it.

Paul said, "Your faith should not stand in the wisdom of men, but in the power of God," for "the weapons of our warfare are not carnal, but mighty *through* God to the pulling down of strongholds" (1 Corinthians 2:5; 2 Corinthians 10:4). No worthy member of the Church ever need suffer enslavement to sins or weaknesses which they, by themselves, cannot overcome, for "the kingdom is given you of the Father, and power to overcome all things which are not ordained of Him" (D&C 50:35).

If your life is not as spiritual and victorious at this time as you wish it were, don't be afraid to look at where you are in your present defeats. Admitting to God where we are in our present defeats is not a *failure*, but a doorway to rebirth and transformation.

CHANGE TAKES TIME

Over the years, many people in the process of recovery from addiction and other problems have asked me how they can know when it is all finally and forever behind them. As important as this question is, it is probably the wrong question.

At the end of a fireside where I had described the transforming, life-saving changes the Savior brought into my life, I was asked if the change in my nature was instantaneous, or if it was a gradual process. My answer to both questions was yes. There was an instant change, a surprising peace, a surprising infusion of power, hope and confidence which came into my being from the moment I finally stopped trying to be my own savior and surrendered to Christ. But there was also a natural process of orderly growth which followed, as He gave me time and experience to make those changes in my character permanent. That process is still going on and I don't expect Him to be done making me whole for a long, long time.

A PROCESS—NOT AN EVENT

Overcoming the desires of the natural man is not easy, and in most cases, it does not come quickly. It only takes a moment or two to surrender and commit our lives to God, but to conquer the flesh requires a lifetime of persistent effort and determination. This process of growth often involves stumbling through bad choices, learning from our mistakes and repenting over and over as we renew our resolves and efforts. "Be not disillusioned by a doctrine of the adversary that there will likely be a magic point in eternity when, all of a sudden, selfish and improper actions will automatically be eliminated from our being" (Robert L. Simpson, *Ensign*, July 1972, p. 49). Since it requires time to perfect our living of those commitments and make them a permanent part of our personality, Christ has instructed: "Ye must *practice* virtue and holiness before me continually" and then asked us to be willing to "continue in patience until ye are perfected" (D&C 46:33; also 38:24; D&C 67:13).

> Behold, ye are little children and ye cannot bear all things now; ye must *grow in grace* and in the knowledge of the truth [D&C 50:40].

Sometimes, in our eagerness to be totally obedient and right with the Lord, we set ourselves up for continued failure and discouragement when we assume that being "born again" or receiving "the mighty change" means that instantly and forever, our battles are over and we no longer have to endure temptation. Someday we will "rest" from the struggle to overcome our weaknesses and sins, but for now, in this mortal testing ground, that is a false, idealistic and unreasonable expectation.

Sometimes we misinterpret the scriptural examples of conversion of people like Paul, Alma and Enos. From such accounts we can know what to reach for and what to expect God to do for us. But those accounts are condensed. They don't tell about the continued struggles and lifetime of growth that occurred after the *starting events* of their conversion. As Elder Merrill J. Bateman said:

> Few mortals share with Alma the Younger or Paul the Apostle the dramatic experiences which resulted in their spiritual rebirths over short periods of time. In fact, I believe those experiences are recorded in the scriptures *not to define the time frame* during which one may be reborn but to provide a vivid picture of what the *accumulated*, subtle changes are that *take place* in a faithful person *over a lifetime* [*Ensign*, Jan. 1999, p. 7].

Thus, for most of us, receiving the mighty change of a new heart and mind is not a miraculous *event*, but more a *process* of gradual improvement and sanctification. It is not reasonable to expect virtue, holiness and victory over our fallen natures to come into our lives from one single choice or event. The battle between the righteous will of our spirit and the desires of our flesh is constant and will be with most of us until we die. No matter how strong and divine the beginning of our "mighty change" and "born again" experience may be, the mental, emotional and physical weaknesses that got us into sin or addiction will never be totally behind us in this life of testing. As President N. Eldon Tanner said: "We must remember that Satan is always on the job, determined to destroy the work of the Lord and to destroy mankind, and as soon as we deviate from the path of righteousness, we are in great danger of being destroyed" (*Ensign*, Dec. 1971, p. 34).

Why would the Savior command, "Let the church take heed and pray always, lest they fall into temptation," (D&C 20:33) if He did not expect us to be vulnerable to temptation throughout our entire mortality? Even after a "born again" experience, we will continue to be subject to temptation, often in the very same ways that we formerly gave in to. I wish that were not so, but it is still that way for me today, even after twenty-five years of being clean—and it is that way for every recovered addict that I have known.

MIRACLES TAKE TIME

The unrealistic expectations of the idea that "I'm-no-good-until-I'm-totally-good" allows Satan to rob us of the transformation and freedom Christ is working to give us. That nearly happened to me back in the early days of writing and speaking at the flood of firesides that followed my first few books, when such experiences were new to me.

I have rarely been given a speaking assignment without being attacked by Satan. Many times it will come in the form of pornography thrust unexpectedly into my path, like someone throwing a magazine over the back fence onto our patio.

On one particular occasion, two pornographic magazines that belonged to the post office box next to mine were misdelivered into my post office box. After a split-second of surprise and hesitation, I rejected the idea of having a look and discarded them without even glancing at the covers. But for the tiniest moment there had been a hesitation of the old curiosity, and Satan used it as a wedge against me. Several days later, as I was preparing a fireside talk, Satan reminded me of it: "*You wanted to look,*" he challenged. "*You are still curious. You haven't really changed. Deep inside, you are still the same, and sooner or later, you are going to go back to it just like you have all the other times in your life.*"

Initially, I did not believe those whisperings. I knew that I had been changed and that I was different now—new and transformed. When such temptations came, I no longer felt compelled to gratify the cravings.

But, because the Lord had been shielding me from the old temptations during the initial months of my rebirth, I had foolishly set myself up with a false expectation of a fairytale-like ending with no more battles. Part of my unrealistic expectation was based on the account of the conversion and transformation of King Benjamin's people. Their testimony had been a major example on which my faith to change and been based, but I had misinterpreted their statement that because the Lord had "wrought a mighty change in us, or in our hearts," they (at the time of that conference with King Benjamin) had "no more disposition to do evil, but to do good continually" (Mosiah 5:2). I had naively assumed that their testimony meant they were no longer tempted or able to be tempted. But that is not what it means, nor is it realistic. I appreciate Stephen E. Robinson's explanation of this scripture:

> From the moment of their conversion, the people of Benjamin changed their orientation and wanted righteousness rather than wickedness. It became their one goal. But that does not mean they achieved their goal instantaneously! It does not mean they never had another carnal thought or that they never subsequently lost any struggle against their carnal natures. At that moment, filled with the Spirit and clearly seeing the two paths before them, the people of Benjamin lost all desire to follow the path of evil. I feel the same way when I feel the Spirit, but I do not always feel the Spirit.
>
> That our disposition is good is proven by the fact that when we occasionally act otherwise, we feel bad about it, repent, and return to our previous heading toward righteousness [*Following Christ,* Salt Lake City, Utah: Deseret Book Co., 1995, pp. 41–42].

I knew that I had experienced some kind of miracle. And because of my idealistic misinterpretation of "no more disposition," those carefully calculated whisperings about me not really being changed did raise doubts in my mind. I couldn't help wondering, if I had truly been "born again," then why had I hesitated for a second or two? Why was the curiosity still there?

As I began to wonder about this challenge to the validity of my rebirth, the demons taunted: "*Who are you to be testifying of the power of Christ to change one's nature when you still have mortal, sinful desires in you?*" As I began to doubt, I began to fear. Not yet understanding that the transformation of our fallen nature is a lifelong process and not a single event, I lost confidence. I began to wonder if my rebirth had indeed been incomplete and imperfect. I began to wonder if I really did have a right to bear witness of the majesty of Christ's infinite power when my changed life was still imperfect. And all this was going on in my mind, not because I had *done* anything wrong, but simply because I had wavered for about two seconds and then been confused by the tauntings of my enemy.

As I allowed myself to give attention to those whisperings, the doubts grew until I almost cancelled all speaking assignments. But before doing that, I had a serious talk with the Lord in which I expressed my confusion and questions. His answer was immediate, strong and clear. The kind words of reprimand came into my mind like thunder. "Who do you think you are, to assume that just because I changed your heart and nature, just because I set you free from your addictions, that you would thereafter coast your way into the celestial kingdom? My Son did not come to earth to skim His way over the surface of life, but tasted every bitter pain and sorrow. His suffering descended below that experienced by any other human. And He had to pay the price until the very last breath. Who do you think you are that it should be any easier for you?"

It was a stern rebuke of my weakness of faith, and misunderstanding of the rebirth I had experienced. Stern, but loving, and it taught me the important truth that it is okay to be human. He taught me that, from time to time, we all grow weary with our struggles and that we all waver in the face of temptation. It is part of the human condition to be imperfect as we move forward on the path toward perfection. I was reminded that even the Savior wavered in the garden when He prayed for an easier way. But Christ's wavering was not counted for sin because He recognized His weakness, prayed for help and then accepted the divine strengthening that was sent. He did His Father's will, completing His mission of atonement. By making sure the apostles recorded that event in the Bible, He set the example of where we can and should turn when we find ourselves wavering and considering a lesser choice.

For a long time I resented my continuing vulnerability to temptation.[1] While I no longer had the desire for pornography or sexual sin, I wanted to be above the temptation and perfect in thought and deed. But now I am grateful for mortal weaknesses which provide me with a constant reminder of how much I need my Savior. I am grateful for the bond that is formed by calling on Him each time I need

---

1 For additional information on this natural man conflict, see Chapter Sixteen, "The Battleground of Perfectionism," in *Putting on the Armor of God*.

strengthening. And most importantly, in this never-ending war that we all face with Satan, I am no longer vulnerable to his vicious lie that because mortals are vulnerable and imperfect, we are not worthy of God's love and are unfit to serve in His kingdom.

Time has demonstrated that my rebirth was genuine. I went on to give that talk and many, many more through the years. The vulnerability to the temptations of pornography is still engrained within me, and just like an alcoholic, I expect my vulnerability to stay with me throughout the rest of my life. While there have continued to be many temptations through the years, God has given me the strength to choose the right.

In this day of fast-food, ATMs and almost everything instant, it is easy to expect too much of ourselves too soon. Remember that in something as life-altering as transforming our fallen natures, the Lord will not be rushed. When we give our life to Him, He will rebuild us for eternity, not just for today, or next week or next year. If He sees fit to take more time to change us than we wish for, we must trust in His wisdom and timing. We must trust that He will grant the changes and transformations we need as quickly as we can be prepared to receive them, because He has promised: "I will order all things for your good, as fast as ye are able to receive them" (D&C 111:11).

WHAT DO I DO?

One of the questions we have frequently received over the years has been, "You keep saying that I must surrender my self will and come to Christ, and I am *willing* to do so, but exactly *how* do I do that?" Likewise, when this began for me, I too, wanted a checklist of instructions—a step-by-step guide to follow. But true spiritual growth doesn't work that way. The "mighty change" does not depend as much on what we do with our outward behavior, as what our *willingness* to improve makes possible for God to do inside us. To receive the mighty change of heart, we need to shift our focus from a comfortable list of things to *do*, so that we can focus on what we need to *be*—or to become.

In school, we may feel overwhelmed with the amount of homework we are assigned, but at least that is something we can see and measure, something we can plan to achieve. In our culture, we are so used to calendars, daily planners and "to-do" checklists, that it is natural for us to want to be in charge. However, the checklist is not up to us. The scriptures never invite us to be in charge of ourselves, but rather to surrender our keeping to the Savior, just as a sheep does to its shepherd, as a child does to its parents, as a tool does to the craftsman, the clay to the potter and even as a branch to the vine.[1] Our part is to give God permission to change us, mold us and to do whatever is required to transform us spiritually, and then to cooperate with Him in the process.

Another reason that neither I nor anyone can provide a simple "A-B-C" or "step 1-2-3" kind of checklist for anyone else is because *how* it needs to happen for one person will never be exactly the same as for

---

1 See examples of these submissive relationships in Alma 5:37-38 and Psalms 100:3; Matthew 18:3 and 3 Nephi 9:22; Isaiah 10:15 and 29:16; Isaiah 64:8 and 45:9; John 15:1-5.)

any other person. The Atonement is personal, not for groups. We are each individual with different sins, weaknesses, backgrounds, hang-ups and needs. Thus, the precise sequential steps of how our transformation will happen, and when it will happen, will be different for each person who is willing to accept the process and allow the Savior to be in charge of it.

Jesus Christ has the knowledge and wisdom to give each person customized tutoring and the power that is needed to escape from the darkness of carnality and confusion into the light, joy, peace and victory of being born again. He knows, to the most intricate detail, the exact path and experiences needed by each person. We are safe in trusting ourselves to Him. It is both exciting and liberating to humbly accept His divine omnipotence and to simply let go and let God be in charge, taking it one step at a time, even without having a clue as to the details of the process or its length.

BUT I STILL DON'T UNDERSTAND!

The most gratifying thing I have learned about the transformation of the second birth is that we do not need to *understand* the process; only to *trust* it and *accept* it. For example, when we need light to eliminate darkness from our homes, we simply flip the light switch. Receiving that light does not depend upon our knowing and understanding the complex process of generating, controlling and delivering electricity to our home. We simply trust the process to work. What we want is a checklist for the rest of our life, but all that we need is to know the next step. (And that is all that Heavenly Father is willing to show any of us, probably because that is how a relationship of trust is built with Him.)

If there were a spiritual switch that we could flip to get the light and guidance we need from Christ, it would have to be found in prayer and the scriptures. Allow me to suggest that a heartfelt, sincere prayer might be the beginning point in your quest for His light to illuminate your next step. Talk to your Heavenly Father about yourself. Remind Him of your struggles and your innermost desires. Confess your unworthiness and great need for Him and His love. Express to Him your recognition that you are powerless to accomplish the change you are seeking without Him. Acknowledge your reliance on the Savior and your gratitude for His sacrifice in your behalf.

Continue to repent each day as thoroughly and sincerely as your limitations will allow. Give yourself, with all your faults, failings, weaknesses and sins to Him with permission to do whatever He knows is best for you. Plead for His love, His forgiveness, and for His guidance.

While you wait for Heavenly Father's response, pray often. Every time you open the scriptures, every time you read the *Ensign*, hear a conference talk, or ponder His blessings, pray that you may find His will for you within those words. Pray morning, noon and night—and listen morning, noon and night.

The surest method of receiving the Lord's guidance is to go to His word, the scriptures, and seek for His personalized answer to you. The messages He would send to you will not necessarily be in the printed word, but may be borne into your heart by the impressions of the Spirit as you ponder them. The specific answers we are seeking may not come immediately, but until they do, we must treasure the principles and promises He has already revealed. Doing so is an act of "flipping the light switch," an invitation for personal revelation. If we show indifference for what He has already said, what right do we have to ask for anything more?

After reading scriptures my entire life, what finally "turned the switch" for me was learning to focus on God's scriptural *promises*. They built my faith enough to make it possible for Him to change me. You may build faith in His promises by reminding God of them, specifically—by chapter and verse—and asking humbly that He will ratify them in your behalf.[2]

In summary, when we need the help of Christ to give us peace or strength to overcome our weaknesses, receiving those divine gifts is not dependent upon our knowledge of how He does that. It depends upon our faith and trust that God knows and that He can and will make it happen for us and within us if we allow it.

> " . . . I will order all things for your good, as fast as ye are able
> to receive them" (D&C 111:11).

---

2 How I went about building my faith in His promises is explained in Appendix C of *Putting On The Armor of God*. Also included there is a listing of about 900 of the most powerful and life-changing promises I found, which the reader could use to start his own arsenal of faith-building spiritual weapons. For additional helps on building faith by claiming God's promises, see also Chapter Eight in *Great Shall Be Your Joy* (pp. 100-105) and "Growing Closer by Claiming The Promises, (pp. 129 – 133) in part two of *In The Arms of His Love*.

UNDERSTANDING DEPRESSION

I've met many people in the Church who suffer feelings of guilt for being depressed. This is not a productive response to depression. With the abundance of medical prescriptions and natural supplements now available for treating depression, the shame should not be in needing emotional or mental support, but rather, in *not doing anything* about it. While I am certainly no authority on the complexities of brain function or mental illness, I have learned some principles for myself that might help those who are struggling with depression.

Until I began my study of depression, I had never thought about the difference between the "mind" and the "brain." I learned that we do not think with the physical brain alone. It is helpful to think of the *mind* as that self-aware part of our eternal spirit that thinks and has consciousness, and to recognize that our *brain* is the physical part of our body that executes, *or carries out the instructions of our conscious mind.* Bruce R. McConkie said, "The sentient, conscious, and intelligent part of man—the part that perceives, feels, wills, and thinks—is called the mind" and "it is clear that the mind of man rests in the eternal spirit. Man's intelligence is in his spirit and not in the natural or mortal body" (*Mormon Doctrine*, Salt Lake City, Utah: Bookcraft, 1966, p. 501).

This means that for every thought we have in our spirit mind, there exists a neurochemical equivalent in the physical brain. Thus, the way we think, the way we feel, and the way we act all happen because of chemical actions in the physical brain—which come in response to the thoughts and instructions coming from the spirit mind. These chemical reactions are dependent upon a complex balance of many separate molecules, working together with specialized brain cells, to communicate and act upon our thoughts, feelings and actions. If that chemical process gets out of balance, so will our thought processes and emotions. In spite of our best intentions, life can become a nightmare.

Being depressed is a little like trying to drive a car with flat tires. While the car could still be driven, it is basically incapacitated and unable to perform as expected. Depression places a similar limitation on relationships. One feels so empty and hollow, so confused, that he cannot relate to people anymore. To escape these complications, he may retreat into isolationism as I did during my sexual addiction years.

After the intense spiritual experience of being rescued and born again, I felt ecstatic. The euphoria I experienced was much like the bouncy happiness one feels during the Christmas season. I felt so wonderful to be free of the threat of falling back into the cycles, so wonderful to feel clean, worthwhile and whole. I had been enjoying a deep and loving fellowship with Deity. I felt that through my books and firesides, I was also helping others gain faith in Christ and find freedom. It was wonderful to feel safe to go home and interact with my wife and children without fear or stress. Our relationships were improving and life was good. I was happy and I felt deep gratitude and devotion to the Lord for saving me, as well as toward LoAnne for her part in that healing process.

But then I began to suffer terribly depressing mood swings. Periodically, I plunged into feelings of dark gloominess, hopelessness and hostility that were very much like I described during the "buffeting" years of my excommunication. Once again that Dr. Jekyll and Mr. Hyde personality was returning. I was confused and bewildered because this time it was not caused by cycles of sin and I didn't know why, or what to do about it. In many ways, those feelings of depression were even worse to deal with than the guilt I had experienced during my years of sin. At least, back then, I had known what to blame. But now, freed from the addictions and immorality, I had no clue what was causing our difficulties. The coming years of depression cycles proved to be as great a threat to our marriage as the addictions had been. It would seem a long time before I got medical help and discovered that what I was suffering has a name and is treatable: clinical depression.

It is not easy to live with a person who suffers from depression. He is often rude, unpleasant, and most annoyingly, irrational and unreasonable. "Because depression changes a person's view of the world, [without his understanding how messed up his thinking process has become] communication becomes difficult and problem solving a challenge" (*Ensign,* October 1996, pp. 49–50).

I discovered that the people who love you too much to let you wallow in your dark, gloomy dungeons can usually be made to keep their distance by pricking them with emotional quills of anger, irritability, rudeness, accusations and hostility. That is what I did to my wife. I was like a confused, angry porcupine.[1] Of course I did not consciously choose to be that way, but it was a way of surviving something that I did not understand.

HOW THE BRAIN WORKS

The physical brain is a collection of 100 billion neurons, or nerve cells, and more than a trillion support cells. These neurons, which make it possible to think, act and feel, are so tiny that they are only one hundredth the size of the period at the end of this sentence. The tentacles which come off the neurons are called dendrites, and the space between them is about one millionth of an inch. These spaces, or microscopic gaps, are called the synapses.

These 100 billion neurons communicate with each other by sending electrical discharges, or "messages," across the synapses, or gaps. But in order for that electrical message to cross a synapse, certain specialized brain chemicals, called neurotransmitters, must travel across this space to trigger a response (chemical reaction) in the target neuron. We could call these neurotransmitters chemical messengers, because they carry every thought and instruction from neuron to neuron—and the brain's function is entirely dependent upon them.

There are hundreds of different neurotransmitter chemicals produced in the brain, and each chemical and transmitter has a different purpose. For example, many neurotransmitters simply carry messages that are received from bodily sensors, relating facts about the outside world, like incoming sounds, patterns of light, temperature, and so forth. Other neurotransmitters carry action messages, such as directing muscles when and how much to move. Still others assist in long-term and short-term memory.

However, there are about 75 neurotransmitters which are the major, controlling ones, which make it possible to think, reason and form conclusions. Some of the best-known neurotransmitters that affect mood and behavior are serotonin, dopamine, and norepinephrine.

---

1 This symbolization is borrowed from a book by Doctor John Lewis Lund: *How To Hug a Porcupine: Dealing With Toxic and Difficult To Love Personalities.* At the time of this rewrite, it is available in most LDS bookstores, at www.amazon.com or www.drlund.com.

WHAT CAUSES DEPRESSION?[2]

The causes of depression can range from an actual disease or medical malfunction in the brain, to more common things like an imbalance or depletion of essential neurotransmitters. If you feel that you may be suffering from depression, it would be wise to seek professional help in determining the cause and best treatment. However, there are certain fundamental roots to this problem that will be helpful to understand as you decide what to do.

The brain consumes about 20 percent of all the energy produced by the food we eat. If we supply the body with proper nutrients, a normal and healthy brain will produce a sufficient and balanced supply of the amino acids which fuel the production of the neurotransmitter chemicals. But if the physical brain chemistry is not healthy and properly balanced, there may be a kind of communication gridlock within the brain, which starts a chain reaction of damaging effects. When this happens, we grow depressed and cannot experience thoughts and feelings the way we should. (Remember the flat tire analogy?)

A depletion or imbalance of neurotransmitter chemicals may result in problems such as feelings of anxiety and depression; irritability and hostility; difficulty sleeping; low energy and chronic fatigue; anger and hopelessness; cravings and insecurity. Life will be confused, as mine was. Our problems, weaknesses and temptations may seem overwhelming and beyond our capacity to overcome. This is one of the reasons that tens of millions of desperate people in America are being medicated with anti-depressant prescriptions—as I was for seventeen years.

Thus, one common problem in our society that puts all of us at risk is the reduction of nutrients in our food chain due to the depletion of minerals in our soil, the use of pesticides and the preponderance of artificial and prepackaged foods. This is why many people have been able to restore a more normal brain chemistry and reduce or eliminate the symptoms of depression with natural supplements that promote a stronger production of the amino acids.[3]

One of the things that gave me courage to make the move to natural supplementation after I had depended upon medical drugs for seventeen years[4] was a statement made by President Ezra Taft Benson.

---

2 For additional information about depression, see the resources listed in Appendix H.

3 A few sources of natural supplementation may be found at
  www.geocities.com/StevenACramer

"Food can affect the mind, and deficiencies in certain elements in the body can promote mental depression. In general, the more food we eat in its natural state and the less it is refined without additives, the healthier it will be for us" (In Conference Report, Oct. 1974, p. 91-92 or "Do Not Despair," *Ensign*, Oct. 1986. p 4). When one considers how far science has advanced since 1974, that was a remarkably insightful statement.

I decided to take responsibility for my own health. I began searching medical journals and health publications for information about brain chemistry and depression. The more I learned, the more sense it made to me that just as we take supplements like Vitamin C and Echinacea to strengthen the immune system, proper nutrients could be taken to strengthen brain chemistry. I am so grateful for the revelations that have advanced medical science and for the rescue that anti–depressants gave me.[5] I am also grateful for scriptures that teach that in many cases, we can treat ourselves with natural remedies God has provided to help keep our bodies healthy (For example, see Alma 46:40; D&C 42:43; 89:10-11).

Abnormal neurochemistries can also be inherited because of defective genetic factors. For example, extensive studies of the children of alcoholics have shown them to share deficiencies in certain neurotransmitters that can cause a predisposition for alcohol that is not experienced by others. Thus, tendencies toward depression can actually "run in families."

In my opinion, the two most common causes of depression among Latter-day Saints stem from satanic attacks and prolonged, unresolved guilt and stress. President Ezra Taft Benson warned of Satan's role: "We live in an age when, as the Lord foretold, men's hearts are failing them, not only physically but in spirit. (See D&C 45:26). "As the showdown between good and evil approaches with its accompanying trials and tribulations, Satan is increasingly striving to overcome the Saints with despair, discouragement, despondency, and depression" ("Do Not Despair," *Ensign*, Oct. 1986, p. 2). [6]

I am not suggesting that Satan can actually cause a clinical, chemical imbalance. I do not know if he is granted that power or not. But I

---

4 Never go off anti-depressant medications suddenly. A gradual reduction taking weeks or months is safest, preferably under a doctor's supervision.

5 If you have concerns about the risks and side effects of chemical prescriptions for your brain, you may wish to review "Mood Altering Drugs" in *Time Magazine*, September 19, 1997.

do know, with absolute certainty, that he and his demons have become masters at using discouragement and depression as a weapon against us. They are also skillful at promoting negative and self-defeating thought patterns that encourage depression because they know that just as one can "overdo" physically, the same thing can happen mentally and emotionally. The way we think affects the way we feel because the neuro-transmitter chemicals are consumed by the brain just as fuel is consumed by a truck. If you require a truck to carry a heavy load up a steep hill, it will consume more fuel than it would on a level road. Similarly, the greater the stress in our lives, the greater the consumption of neurotransmitters in our fragile brain chemistry. That is why many people experience temporary bouts of depression when confronted with major stress events like loss of a job or a loved one.

Many times we simply talk ourselves into or out of depression. There are physical and scientific reasons for commandments and statements of principle like, "Let your hearts rejoice, and be exceedingly glad," (D&C 128:22) and "a merry heart doeth good like a medicine" (Proverbs 17:22). It is common knowledge that laughter and positive thoughts promote the production of beneficial hormones and brain function, while negative thoughts diminish them. People can easily cause themselves to have gloomy, depressive thoughts and feelings simply by focusing on the discouraging and unwanted circumstances in their lives.[7]

> When discouragement weighs heavily, look around again. Recognize discouragement for what it is: one of Satan's subtlest yet most devastating tools. He would convince us that we are unworthy of respect or affection, enticing us to wallow in the mire of self-pity [Anne G. Osborn, *Ensign*, Mar. 1977, p. 49].

Those kinds of mood swings, or "downers," usually pass as we regain control of our attitude. But a prolonged stress of unresolved problems, like the thirty years of guilt, financial debt, marriage problems and hopelessness that I struggled through can lead to a serious chemical imbalance and depression. It is a natural physical response.

---

6 "Through prayer and scripture study, I learned that the source of my depression was Satan and that his influence can be overcome by going to the Lord for help and then acting upon the impressions received" (Janet Nelson Christensen, *Ensign*, Aug. 1996, p. 53).

7 Elder Joseph B. Wirthlin said: "We should seek to be happy and cheerful and not allow Satan to overcome us with discouragement, despair, or depression" (*Ensign*, May 1992, p. 87).

It is my opinion that if someone is trying to grow spiritually and conquer inappropriate emotional or behavioral problems—but have an untreated chemical imbalance—they are fighting with both hands tied behind their backs and with unnecessary and almost insurmountable handicaps. As one nutritional scientist stated: "Building toward effective self-actualization cannot use a short-cut approach. If we demand behavior change from our clients without allowing rebalancing of brain chemistry, we simply set them up for failure" ("Neuronutrient Therapy" by Doctor Terry Neher, *Professional Counselor Magazine*, Aug. 1993, p.53).

NATURAL SUPPLEMENTATION OR MEDICAL PRESCRIPTION?

Brain chemistry is fragile and complex. Treating depression is not simple. Just as one single optical prescription for eyeglasses will not correct everyone's vision, no single medication or supplement can balance everyone's brain chemistry. The only way a person can find a mood-altering medication or supplement that will work for them is to patiently give it a try and then let the body report back if it feels better. Whether you decide to put a doctor in charge of prescribing your medication, or try to find the proper supplementation yourself, it usually takes weeks or months of trial to find the medication or supplement that will work best and then more time to determine the proper dosage.

In our quest for spiritual and mental health, there will be many hills to ascend. Don't assume that you must do so with "flat tires" without at least investigating the many avenues that are now available for treatment.

Gerald

RESOURCES FOR RECOVERY AND SUPPORT

THE ADDICTION RECOVERY PROGRAM

The Church's Family Services department is providing an effective 12 step recovery program to assist members desiring to overcome various addictions, such as substance abuse, pornography, compulsive overeating or gambling.

Support group meetings are led by Church service missionaries under the direction of local LDS Family Services agencies and priesthood leaders. They are achieving wonderful results, both for those in addiction and for the support of confused and heart-broken family members.

While it is possible, through the aid of the Savior, for an individual to recover from addiction without the aid of such a program, time and experience has proven that working on such problems in a group and with the structure of the "12 Steps" is usually far more rapid and lasting. How I wish such training and experience been available to help me during my struggles.

To locate the nearest **Addiction Recovery Program**, call LDS Family Services at **(800) 453-3860**, extension **2-3646**. (If there is no support group operating within a reasonable distance in your area, you might request your stake president to confer with the local LDS Family Services agency about starting a group in that area.)

ONLINE INTERNET SOURCES OF HELP

In the war for our souls that is waged here on earth, Satan and his demons are constantly trying to fill us with lies and rob us of knowledge, while our Heavenly Father, the Savior and the Holy Ghost are working to bring light and truth into our minds and hearts, for it is "the truth [that] shall make you free" (See John 8:32; D&C 84:10; 93:39).

The scriptures, the teachings of Church leaders and personal revelation are our primary sources of saving truths, but we should also seek wisdom and knowledge from every possible source.

Technology is hastening the Lord's work in these last days and the following web sites are but a few of the many good sites that can provide many talks and articles explaining truths that will be valuable to those seeking recovery from addiction, as well as those who are attempting to support them.

On the Church's Family Services Web site that is available at **http://providentliving.org** you will find a wide range of resources on mental, emotional and spiritual health issues, ranging from abuse and anger management, to marriage and divorce, self-esteem, stress management, pornography, substance abuse and even same-sex attraction issues. On the home page, first click on "Social and Emotional Strength," and then click on "Library of Helpful Information."

BYU's Web site, at **http://www.byu.edu** also provides a wide range of resources on mental, emotional and spiritual health issues, including dozens of articles on pornography and sexual addiction. On the home page, first click on the "search" link, and then type "pornography" (or whatever subject you wish to access), in the search window.

Doctor James Dobson's "Focus On The Family" Web site **http://www.family.org** provides strong Christian support on pornography's effect on the individual, marriage and family. Just type "pornography" in the home page search window.

An excellent Christ-centered 12-step recovery and support group for Church members struggling with various forms of addiction and compulsive behaviors is Heart t'Heart, formed by Latter-day Saint lay members. To access the locations of their support group meetings, or resource materials, just click on: **http://www.heart-t-heart.org**

The most complete resource site and organization for helping Latter-day Saints struggling to overcome same-sex attractions is found at: **http://www.evergreen-intl.org/** This organization believes that individuals can overcome homosexual behavior and diminish same-sex attraction and is committed to assisting individuals who wish to do so.

For additional resources and links recommended by the author, please visit his Web Site at:

http://www.geocities.com/StevenACramer

BOOKS AND FIRESIDES
BY STEVEN A. CRAMER:

Putting On The Armor of God—Book [Springville, Utah: Cedar Fort] To win your battles, you must know your enemy. This book contains a detailed analysis of the cunning devices, manipulations, strategies of defeat and temptation used by Satan to rob us of purity, hope and determination. It includes step-by-step strategies for increasing faith and protecting ourselves on the battlegrounds of thought, morals, prayer, temptations, memories, perfectionism, and others by drawing upon the armor of God and His grace and power to defend ourselves and win our battles.

Conquering Your Own Goliaths—Book [Springville, Utah: Cedar Fort] Illustrates that the Lord is always at the ready to deliver us from even the most serious of circumstances. Explains how to apply the Atonement to overcome common self-defeating spiritual Goliaths, such as poor self-image, improper thought habits, temptations, adversity, unresolved guilt and indecision.

"Conquering Your Own Goliaths"—Fireside cassette recording [American Fork, Utah: Covenant Communications]. Summarizes key points from the book on how to face our challenges more effectively by drawing on the power of Christ.

Great Shall Be Your Joy—Book [Springville, Utah: Cedar Fort] This book explains how to draw upon Christ's power and grace to compensate for our weaknesses; how to partner with Him in the struggles to overcome our fallen natures instead of trying to be our own savior; how to be more submissive and trusting in God's promises to us, and develop a Christ-centered foundation that will lead us into true righteousness and spiritual victory.

In The Arms of His Love—Book and full text cassette recording

[American Fork, Utah: Covenant Communications]. An assurance of the Savior's infinite and unconditional love and concern for every person, regardless of their present lifestyle. How to overcome the barriers that prevent us from believing and accepting His love; plus nine specific strategies for how to draw closer to God, share His love more effectively with others, and eventually meet Him face to face.

Draw Near Unto Me—Book and full text cassette recording [American Fork, Utah: Covenant Communications] Twenty-five strategies for overcoming the most common barriers that keep us from coming to Christ, having more faith in Him and becoming more like Him.

In His Image—Book and fireside cassette recording [American Fork, Utah: Covenant Communications]. You can increase the power of your eternal spirit over the limitations of your body and natural man condition simply by improving the use of each part of your physical body. The task of making temples of our bodies, and becoming more like the Savior, is made easier by the strategies provided for gaining control of each major part of the body, such as the mouth, the mind and heart, the eyes, ears and hands.

"Winning the Battles with Satan"—Fireside cassette recording [American Fork, Utah: Covenant Communications]. Describes exactly how Satan attacks and manipulates our thoughts and feelings and how we can protect ourselves from him.

"Angels: Messengers of God's Love"—Fireside recording on cassette or CD [American Fork, Utah: Covenant Communications]. Some of the topics in this talk include: Who are angels? Where do they live? What do they do? What do they look like? What are their powers? What are the different types of angels? Are there really "guardian angels?" What do we need to do to qualify for the promptings or ministering of angels in our lives?

BOOKS AND CASSETTE RECORDINGS BY OTHER AUTHORS

I have found each of the following books, recordings or articles of personal value in my own quest.

He Did Deliver Me From Bondage, [Colleen C. Harrison, Pleasant Grove, Utah: Windhaven Publishing. Available in LDS bookstores, or at **http://www.rosehavenpublishing.com**]. This self-guiding workbook merges the time-tested principles from the original 12 steps of Alcoholics Anonymous, which have helped millions to recover from that addiction, with the gospel principles of repentance, forgiveness and spiritual transformation, as revealed in Latter-day Saint scriptures. It identifies many of the self-defeating assumptions so many Latter-day Saints make about having to obey everything perfectly, on their own, in order to be acceptable to God. It presents compelling instructions on how to believe, accept and draw upon the promises Christ has made to help us overcome the weaknesses we cannot conquer by ourselves. While intended to be used in 12 step support groups, it can also be used individually.

Turn Yourselves and Live, [Rod W. Jeppsen, Sandy, Utah: Vescorp]. This book also helps the reader to identify the root problems in compulsive sexual addictions. It provides hope and practical guidance to those who are struggling with a compulsive sexual lifestyle as well as to the individuals who are trying to help them get out of such behavior. The workbook format helps the reader to get out of denial, distinguish the difference between irrational thoughts and rational Christ-centered thoughts and shows them how to defuse "trigger points" that perpetuate the addiction.

Believing Christ and *Following Christ*, [Stephen E. Robinson, Salt Lake City, Utah: Desert Book Company]. Two excellent books for learning to believe and claim the promises of Christ in our lives. How to bridge the doubts and hang-ups of perfectionism that keep so many from fully coming to Christ and receiving the transforming power of His divine grace.

Grace Works, [Robert L. Millet, Salt Lake City, Utah: Deseret Book Company]. Of the "after all we can do" dilemma, he says: "The grace of God is more than just a final boost into celestial glory…"(p. 144). This book brilliantly bridges the gap between the natural man pride of self-sufficiency that often prevents the Lord from assisting us in our efforts, and the need we all share for the divine aid His grace provides in partnering with our righteous intentions.

The Miracle of Forgiveness, [Spencer W. Kimball, Salt Lake City: Bookcraft] While stern and uncompromising in its condemnation of sin, this book is filled with hope, encouragement and the promise of divine help for every person who is ready and willing to repent. It explains why the sinner is suffering and shows the pathway out of that pain to forgiveness and peace.

Willpower is Not Enough, [A. Dean Byrd and Mark Chamberlain, Salt Lake City, Utah: Deseret Book Company]. This book explains why real change requires more than determination and why willpower often prevents change more than helping it. It tells how to get past the limitations of the mind and draw upon the stronger power of the heart and emotions. Each principle is illustrated by compelling case studies about the dilemmas and recoveries of real people.

Drawing Upon The Powers of Heaven, [Grant Von Harrison, Provo, Utah: The *Ensign* Publishing Company]. This book is excellent for learning the principles and practical procedures involved in making one's faith and prayers more effective.

"How To Be Chaste While Being Chased," Fireside on audio cassette or CD [Curtis Jacobs, American Fork, Utah: Covenant Communications]. Excellent and fun discussion for both youth and adults about the attitudes, boundaries and discipline required to withstand moral temptations while dating and forming relationships.

How To Hug a Porcupine, [Doctor John Lewis Lund, The Communications Company at http://www.drlund.com]. This book is very helpful for learning how to deal with toxic people who make it difficult to love them or get along with them. It provides excellent ideas for how to improve relationships without intruding upon their agency, as well as how to protect our feelings from the hurts they might otherwise inflict on us.

All the products listed above are available at LDS bookstores, or online.

http://www.cedarfort.com

http://www.deseretbook.com/store

http://www.seagullbook.com

http://www.covenant-lds.com

ARTICLES FROM CHURCH MAGAZINES:

> The articles listed below are now available on line at
> **http://www.lds.org**
>
> First click on the Directory Topic of "Gospel Library"
> Then click on "Search the Data Base"
> Then click on "Magazines"
> This will give you access to the last thirty years of Church
> Magazine articles

COMING MORE FULLY TO THE SAVIOR

"Come unto Christ," President Ezra Taft Benson, *The New Era*, April 1988, pp. 4-7.

"A Mighty Change of Heart," President Ezra Taft Benson, *Ensign*, Oct. 1989, pp. 2-5.

"Jesus Christ—Gifts and Expectations," Elder Ezra Taft Benson, *The New Era*, May 1975, pp. 16-21.

"Jesus Christ—Our Savior and Redeemer," Ezra Taft Benson, *Ensign*, June 1990, pp. 2-6.

"Five Marks of the Divinity of Jesus Christ," Ezra Taft Benson, *The New Era*, Dec. 1980, pp. 44-50.

"Toward a Mature Discipleship," Karen Lynn Davidson, *Ensign*, July 1984, pp. 45-47.

"Journey Toward Righteousness," A. Lynn Scoresby, *Ensign*, Jan. 1980, pp. 53-56.

DEALING WITH PORNOGRAPHY AND ISSUES OF IMMORALITY

"Breaking the Chains of Pornography," *Ensign*, Feb. 2001, pp. 55-59.

"You Can't Pet a Rattlesnake," Elder David E. Sorensen, *Ensign*, May 2001, p. 41-42.

"Personal Purity," Elder Jeffrey R. Holland, *Ensign*, Nov. 1998, pp. 75-78.

"Pornography, the Deadly Carrier," *Ensign*, July 2001, p. 2-5.

"Leave the Obscene Unseen," R. Gary Shapiro, *Ensign*, Aug. 1989, pp. 27-29.

"Pollution of the Mind," Robert L. Simpson, *Ensign*, Jan. 1973, pp. 112-113.

"Overpowering the Goliaths in Our Lives," Gordon B. Hinckley, *Ensign*, May 1983, pp. 46-52.

"Idea List: Clean Thoughts," *The The New Era*, Feb. 2001, p.15.

"Being Clean Again," *Ensign*, Sep. 1996, pp. 20-22.

DEALING WITH DEPRESSION

"Why Is My Wife (Or Husband) Depressed?" David G. Weight, *Ensign*, Mar. 1990, p. 27-29.

"'Awake My Soul!': Dealing Firmly with Depression," Steve Gilliland, *Ensign*, Aug. 1978, 37-41.

"When Life Is Getting You Down," Val D. MacMurray, Ph.D., *Ensign*, June 1984, p. 56-60.

"Escaping My Valley of Sorrow," G. G.Vandagriff, *Ensign*, March 2000, pp. 65-67.

"My Battle with Depression," Mollie H. Sorensen, *Ensign*, Feb. 1984, p.12-16.

"Rising Above the Blues," Shanna Ghaznavi, *The New Era*, Apr. 2002, p. 30-34.

SAVING OUR MARRIAGE AND FAMILY

"Mending Our Marriage," *Ensign*, Oct. 1996, pp. 44-51.

"To Help a Loved One In Need," Elder Richard G. Scott, *Ensign*, May 1988, pp. 60-61.

"A Time To Heal," Lynn Clark Scott, *Ensign*, April 1989, pp. 56-59.

"Healing Soul and Body," Elder Robert D. Hales, *Ensign*, Nov. 1998. pp. 14-17.

"The Pitfalls of Parallel Marriage," Charles B. Beckert, *Ensign,* Mar. 2000, pp. 22-25.

"To Forgive is Divine," Theodore M. Burton *Ensign,* May 1983, pp. 70-72.

UNDERSTANDING CHURCH DISCIPLINE

"Courts of Love," Robert L. Simpson, *Ensign,* July, 1972, pp. 48-49.

" To Bear The Priesthood Worthily," Spencer W. Kimball, May 1975, *Ensign,* pp. 78-81.

"Let Mercy Temper Justice," Theodore M. Burton, *Ensign,* Nov. 1985, 64-66.

"Cast Your Burden Upon the Lord," Robert L. Simpson, *The New Era,* Jan. 1977, pp. 4-8.

"Justice and Mercy," James A. Cullimore, *Ensign,* May 1974, pp. 29-31.

A LETTER OF LOVE

My wife was blessed with celestial parents. During the stress of my dropping out of church and threatening to leave home, she made a trip to visit them seeking courage and help to save our marriage. Her parents could have easily and justifiably been angry and resentful toward me, but their concern was as great for my peril as it was for their daughter's. Her father wrote a letter to me and sent it home with LoAnne. It had a profound effect upon me. More than anything else that happened, this insightful letter made me hesitate in the downward path I was taking. It contains some great lessons:

Dear Gerald,

We have been enjoying our daughter's visit and are thankful she came. I want to let you know again that we love you and respect you for many of the very fine things you do, and have done, and for the very fine person we know you to be. I want you to know of our love and keep it in mind during the next few minutes as you read this letter. Sometimes we need to hear more than just love, and it is in my heart to say some rather strong things to you, but in love and understanding, and with the hope that you will open your heart to it and accept it as trying to help you rather than to chastise you.

The course you are now taking can result in serious self-doubts. I mean the bit about not praying, not attending your Church duties with wholehearted participation. I don't know why you are doing this. Perhaps you don't either. But ask yourself with your usual honesty if it could be that by withholding yourself, you are trying to reprimand God for what He is allowing to happen to you.

Our daughter says you say you still know the Church is true, but that you seem to have given up caring. When a child is thus disappointed he picks up his marbles and goes home in protest. When will you pick up again, if ever? Will it be after God changes some of the conditions of your life you now resent? And suppose those conditions do not improve. What is the next logical step to follow? Is it to take up sin? I know of children who get back at their parents by such behavior. By extension I see it possible to do the same with God, our Father. We could say to Him, "Very well, if you do not care about me, then I don't care about myself or You."

I recall that although I paid my tithing and lived the gospel fairly well, I had nothing but problems on the farm I bought. After a large down payment and all I had put into it, grubbing out the mesquite trees, leveling it, drilling a well, I had nothing but problems. For example, after a hailstorm that knocked out half of my first crop, my second year brought a sharp freeze. My farm was the only one in the valley that was seriously damaged by the hailstorm, and it happened while I was in Salt Lake City to General Conference. The second year's cotton crop had been examined by several competent men as in excess of $30,000 worth of cotton. After the frost I picked less than $6,000 worth. Then to make matters worse, the government decided to ration cotton the next year, but hadn't announced how drastic it was to be. Hence, no bank was willing to lend money. A year earlier I could have borrowed $10,000 with no difficulty. At this time I couldn't even borrow $2,500, which would have been more than enough to save my farm. Also, the company I had purchased my cotton-picker from got upset with the conditions and repossessed it.

When I worked at the ice plant, I took over a defunct milk business, built it up to a respectable income, bought the ice plant and three houses for $100,000. It had been earning $25,000 yearly in ice sales. I had hardly made the transaction before the state moved the truck weighing scales from the state line eighteen miles to the west to the east side of town. A truck could no longer ice up as before because they had to keep weight down till they could pass the scales. Many were the trucks that stopped needing 3,000 to 4,000 pounds of ice, but couldn't buy it because they had to cross the scales. As my business died, I lost the ice plant after paying $40,000 on it.

Because I wrote a letter published in the newspaper decrying dishonest practices in the town's service stations, certain of the disgruntled men wrote letters to the milk company I worked for which were bitterly biased. They got employees in the stores to put some of my milk out in the sun for a day, then back in the store to sell to the customers as sour. Everything that could be done to cause me to fail was done.

During all this time I was in the bishopric. My boys and I practically kept the ward and its welfare and budget by cutting and bailing paper hay and doing 80 percent of the irrigating and hoeing on the church farm. I sent three of them on missions, overlapping their terms twice. It would have been easy to lose heart and give up and quit. I told the Lord I was thankful for my blessings. Only one house burned down. We still had our health, our testimony, and the children were turning out to be true Latter-day Saints. I had much for which to be thankful. Not only so, but during the fire I burned my feet so badly getting the little girls out that the doctors told me I would have to have skin grafted on my feet. The bishop and my son gave me a blessing, and my feet healed without even a scar. I know I was blessed in my misfortune.

I leased the "180 Camp" which included a store, a service station, and 20 rental cabins. I had it only a month when they bypassed the highway around me for over a year while they built an underpass and cloverleaf to enter the freeway. You can imagine what that did to my business for a year as the rent went on just the same.

Now I've outlined some of the things that have happened to me. Not to make anyone sorry for poor little me, but to point out that the things in life which really count have always been in my favor. It began to look like I would never succeed at anything and would always have my nose at the grindstone. Until the last year or two I have never been out of debt. And we had eight children to raise with me being the only breadwinner. I know how hopeless it can look at times. However, my misfortunes could have been so much worse. My children never missed a meal nor were they poorly clothed nor suffered any serious misfortune. Through it all we were highly blessed.

Remember the section in the Doctrine and Covenants where the prophet felt he had borne too much, and he was told by the Lord that his misfortunes were but for a moment and, if faithful, what great rewards were promised. That promise is to all who will endure to the end. We are not promised a life of ease or trouble-free existence. Instead, this mortal life was designed to give us the troubles by which we can grow.

Now, as I look at your life, I don't see anything so terrible or world-shaking. You have lived with the respect and love of your fellow-members. I doubt your family has often gone hungry. They all have brilliant minds and faithful hearts. You have great reason to rejoice in the blessings Heaven has sent you. If you can't be thankful for these great blessings, you may be asking for more serious troubles to chastise and humble you. The sin of ingratitude is great.

I have admired the way you have kept at the job of providing for your family, and you have had a lot of the "experience" the Lord told Joseph Smith he was getting. Don't give up yet or get to feeling sorry for yourself.

When I gave you my daughter, I didn't think life would be easy for you. But I didn't think you would be a quitter. When she came to me some years ago to see if she should leave you because you were not getting along well together and had problems, I advised her to go back and work it out together, and your super children would be a prize beyond value you could earn together. I have not wavered in that belief—I see it ever stronger today.

Now, my son, lift yourself out of your morass of troubles and be thankful for what you have. Ask the Lord to forgive you for temporarily losing sight of your great blessings. Lose yourself in service to others, and you will find great happiness in this life and eternal joy in the world to come. If you do not do this, I fear you will lose your testimony and be delivered to the buffetings of Satan. And if you think your lot has been hard, it will become vastly much more so and with little hope for eternal reward. How bitter is servitude to the devil!

Don't overwork yourself to the point of exhaustion. In so doing you lose your perspective. Take time for the Sabbath. The example to your family is too precious to lose. God will fulfill his promise to open the windows of heaven and pour out blessings. These may not be largely financial, but you will be taken care of. You have a wife and family who will stick with you and without complaint. These are blessings beyond the reach of many. Look at your financial struggles as opportunities, for that is what they are. Some of my happiest years were spent with my nose continually at the grindstone.

Learn to live each day for itself. In other words, there is joy you are now missing that could be yours with only a change of attitude. Attitude is so important in finding joy. Do not look forward to different conditions to bring you joy. You will lose it in the searching. It could be yours right now and in your present circumstances if you can so order your thinking to embrace it. These are not just empty platitudes. They can and will work. They have done so for me, and I can promise you in the name of Israel's God they can work for you. If they are not now doing so, it is the fault of your attitude.

This has been a long letter. Perhaps I have missed the point. But I have tried in love to help you and raise your perspectives. I sympathize with you in your troubles, but remind you they are what you shouted for joy with Job to receive. They are what you came here for. Make the most of them or your blessings can be taken away. We love you, and we gave you our daughter. She is a prize worth a pearl of any great price. Cleave unto her. Your marriage is no worse than many and better than most, and it can be just what you are willing to pay for it.

I could say this so much better to you if we were together. I am no great sage, or terribly wise, but there are some things I know truly, and one is that you have been and are being greatly blessed. Don't slack off in the effort to live the gospel. You will find out in great bitterness that you punished only yourself and not God if you let up now. And to the end you may do so, we earnestly pray for you. And send our love.

As ever,